I0901806

PUBLIC ENGAGEMENT IN THE EUROPEAN MIDDLE AGES

TEACHING THE MIDDLE AGES

Further Information and Publications

www.arc-humanities.org/series/book-series/

PUBLIC ENGAGEMENT IN THE EUROPEAN MIDDLE AGES

MEDIEVAL SOLUTIONS FOR A MODERN CRISIS

by

CHRISTOPHER D. FLETCHER

ARC HUMANITIES PRESS

British Library Cataloguing in Publication Data
A catalogue record for this book is available from the British Library.

© 2025, Arc Humanities Press, Leeds

This work is licensed under a Creative Commons Attribution-NonCommercial-NoDerivatives 4.0 International Licence.

The author(s) assert(s) their moral right to be identified as the author(s) of their part of this work.

Permission to use brief excerpts from this work in scholarly and educational works is hereby granted provided that the source is acknowledged. Any use of material in this work that is an exception or limitation covered by Article 5 of the European Union's Copyright Directive (2001/29/EC) or would be determined to be "fair use" under Section 107 of the U.S. Copyright Act September 2010 Page 2 or that satisfies the conditions specified in Section 108 of the U.S. Copyright Act (17 USC §108, as revised by P.L. 94-553) does not require the Publisher's permission.

ISBN (Hardback): 9781802700961
ISBN (Paperback): 9781802703849
e-ISBN (PDF): 9781802703832
e-ISBN (EPUB): 9781802703825

www.arc-humanities.org

Printed and bound in the UK (by CPIGroup [UK] Ltd), USA (by Bookmasters), and elsewhere using print-on-demand technology.

Publisher (manufacturer) details: Arc Humanities Press, 14 Clifton Moor Business Village, James Nicolson Link, York YO30 4XG, United Kingdom.

EU Authorized Representative details (for GPSR purposes): Amsterdam University Press, Nieuwe Prinsengracht 89, 1018 VR Amsterdam, The Netherlands. www.aup.nl

CONTENTS

LIST OF ILLUSTRATIONS

Figures

Table

For Stephanie, Theo, and Grace

PREFACE

GREETINGS! WELCOME TO *Public Engagement in the European Middle Ages: Medieval Solutions for a Modern Crisis*. Thanks for taking the time to read this book; I hope you find it useful.

Before we get started, I have a couple of orders of business. While I love footnotes as much as the next medievalist, I decided to keep them to a minimum in this book by using in-line citations for the most frequently-used sources. Each one of these is a little different, so you'll find specific details about how the various citations work early on in each chapter. Also, all the translations in this book are my own, unless otherwise noted.

Now that that's out of the way, I can get to the more important part: thanking the many people who have helped make this book a reality over the years. First, to Danna Messer, Tania Colwell, and the rest of the staff at Arc Humanities Press, thank you for taking a chance on this book and providing all the sound guidance and encouragement a first-time author (like me) needed.

Second, to Dr. Elizabeth Harding, Dr. Volker Bauer, and the librarians, staff, and fellows at the Herzog August Bibliothek in Wolfenbüttel: thank you for awarding me a short-term fellowship at the HAB in the summer of 2023, for giving me access to your collections, and for welcoming me into your vibrant intellectual community that made it possible for me to finish the first draft of this book.

Speaking of funding, I owe special gratitude to the Newberry Library's Fellowships department and anonymous reviewers for awarding this book the Weiss-Brown Publication Subvention Award, which supports the publication of outstanding works of scholarship that cover European civilization before 1700 in the areas of music, theatre, French or Italian literature, or cultural studies. It is made to commemorate the career of Howard Mayer Brown.

Next up are the good people in the Honors College at the University of Illinois at Chicago, where I've had the pleasure of teaching an undergraduate core course on public engagement in medieval Europe since 2021. To the Honors College administration and staff—especially Michele McCrillis and Yolanda Rodriguez-Venegas—thank you for the opportunity to teach this course and for taking care of all the logistical details to make it happen. And, of course, to all my students, thank you for being engaged, patient, and willing participants in what turned out to be a multi-year process of workshopping the case studies in the following pages.

And now for the many academic colleagues—graduate students, faculty, and independent scholars—with whom I've worked out my thoughts about public engagement and medieval Europe in classes, programs, and conversations. To all of you, thank you for pushing me to make my arguments stronger and assuring me that what I thought I was seeing in medieval culture was really there. In particular, to Bryan Brazeau, Kristen Haas Curtis, Elisa Jones, Isabella Magni, and Anne Koening, thank you all for helping me work through my struggles with academia and for showing me a different way to think about the accessibility of medieval culture. Lastly, to Becky Fall, Liz Hebbard, and Jonathan Lyon, thank you for taking the time to do all the above and read and respond to earlier drafts of this book.

That brings me to all my wonderful colleagues, past and present, at the Newberry Library in Chicago, several of whom you'll meet a bit later on. To all the staff in Collections and Library Services, thank you for making it so easy both to work with the Newberry's medieval collections and to share them with all kinds of audiences over the years. To my compatriots in Research and Education (especially the crew in 4-East), thank you for humouring me as I shoehorned medieval content into every possible conversation and, more importantly, for showing every day how it's possible to use academic expertise to make a difference in the world through your inspiring work. It has been a blessing to work with you all, but I have to single out two in particular for their role in making this book happen. To Kara Johnson, thank you for showing what compassionate pedagogy looks like and for being the first person to read and respond to this book. And, above all, to the Director of the Center for Renaissance Studies, Lia Markey: thank you for your vision, your wisdom, your leadership, and your encouragement to always "just go for it." I can only hope that this book embodies just a tiny piece of the transformative culture you've created.

Finally, we come to the most important thanks of all. To my parents and sisters, thank you for the constant and unshakeable support (and relatively small number of eye rolls) you've given me as I've tried to understand and explain why medieval people did what they did. But most of all, to Stephanie, Theo, and Grace: thank you for being the unending source of the patience, steadfastness, and love I needed to finish this journey. This book is for you guys.

Soli Deo gloria.
Chicago, October 2024

INTRODUCTION

Back in the fall of 2019, I had the strangest epiphany of my professional career. This lightning bolt moment came one afternoon in the Special Collections reading room at the Newberry Library, where I was looking at an old book with my friend and colleague Federica Caneparo, a brilliant scholar of Italian art and literature in sixteenth-century Italy. We were there so Federica could introduce me to the 1522 edition of Ovid's *Metamorphoses*.[1] This was the first Italian translation of Ovid's masterwork to be printed, and the publisher, Niccolò Zuppino, wanted to help it make a big splash by adding a nearly full-page woodcut portrait of the Roman author to adorn the title page (Fig. 1). According to Federica, Zuppino wanted this portrait to make clear that the volume embraced the spirit of the Renaissance by showing Ovid with the full iconography of an ancient poet (and not, she was clear, a medieval doctor) hard at work in his study. However, as soon as I laid eyes on this woodcut, I *immediately* thought: "Oh my gosh, that's medieval studies."

Even *I* was confused by this gut reaction. Why on earth would I think that? I had no idea, and, slightly embarrassed, I didn't say anything about it to Federica at the time. Over the rest of the day, though, I kept trying to figure out why I would think this Renaissance depiction of a first-century Roman poet immediately struck me as the perfect visualization of my field. It could have been the fact that the portrait shows Ovid toiling away on a no-doubt important and interesting intellectual project that required consulting cool old books, which resonated with a lot of things I liked about being a professional medievalist. But no, that wasn't it. After a while, I realized that what struck a chord with me had nothing to do with what Ovid was doing, but with how he seemed to be *feeling*. In that image I saw not a proud ancient laureate, but sad and resigned scholar, with his head resting heavily in his hand while staring out the open window with empty eyes. For me, this title page did not show an influential, successful intellectual, but a

1 Publius Ovidius Naso, *Tutti gli libri de Ouidio Metamorphoseos* (Venice: Niccolò Zuppino, 1522), Chicago, The Newberry Library, Case Y 672 .09647.

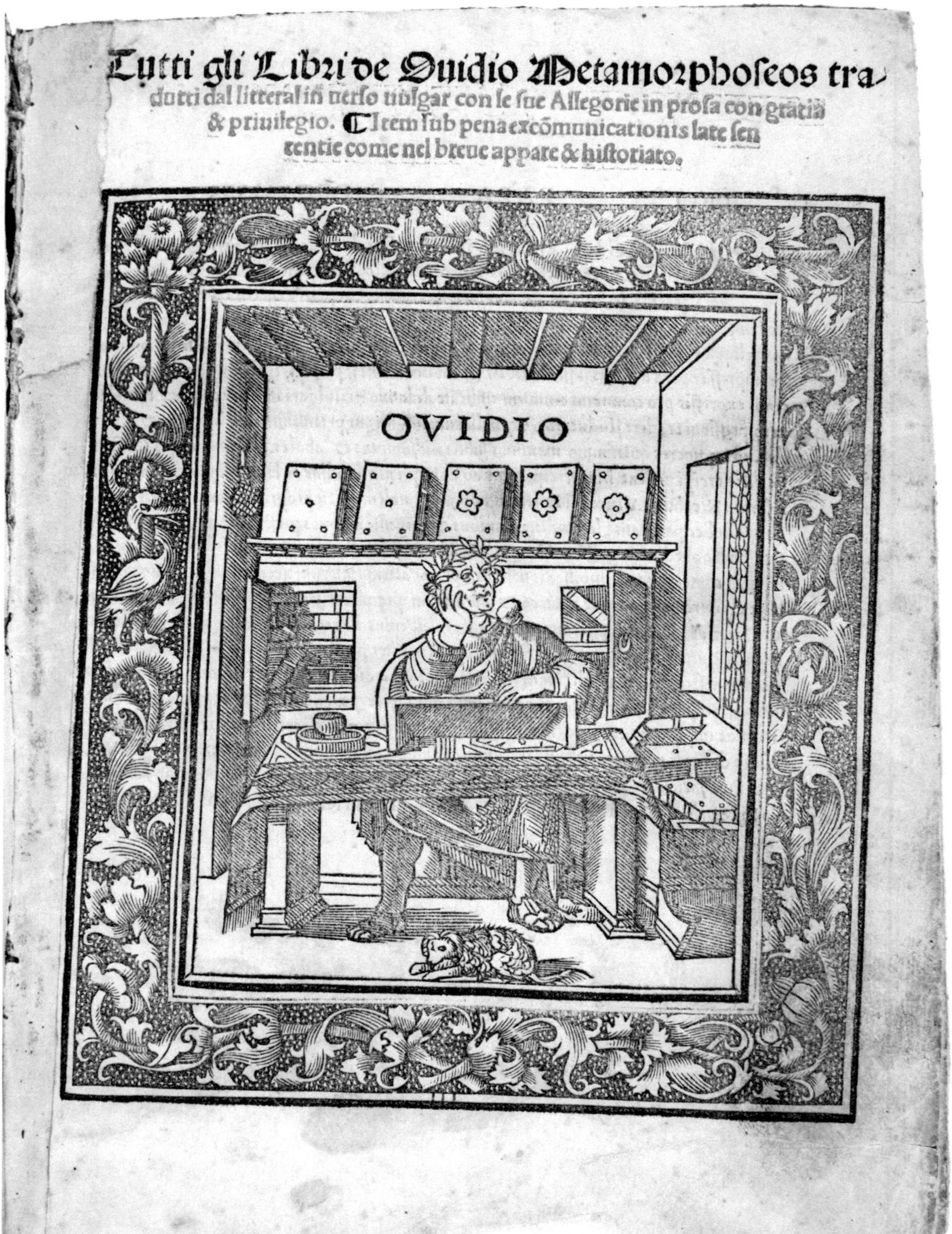

Figure 1. "Sad Ovid" woodcut on the title page of Publius Ovidius Naso, *Tutti gli libri de Ouidio Metamorphoseos* (Venice: Niccolò Zuppino, 1522). Chicago, The Newberry Library, Case Y 672 .O9647. Open Access. Courtesy of the Newberry Library.

melancholy man who, despite his important project and his cool old books, sat sadly pondering why he was sitting in his study all alone.

In that sense, "Sad Ovid" (as I now call him) seemed like the perfect visualization of the current state of the field of medieval studies. If you're reading this book, I assume that you're already well aware of the ongoing "crisis of the humanities" and how hard it seems to have hit medieval studies in particular. We don't need to rehash all the gory details here; I imagine most every medievalist has personally experienced the field's steadily eroding institutional presence, its growing inability to secure financial support from institutions or granting organizations, its ever-shrinking graduate cohorts, and its increasingly constricting job market.[2] If all this continues, the field faces a *very* uncertain future, to say the least, and everybody—whether they're a medievalist or not—knows it.

This whole unfortunate situation has stirred up some pretty intense emotions from medievalists in the early twenty-first century. It was those emotions—loneliness, isolation, and profound anxiety about the future—that I read in Sad Ovid's face. While there are plenty of things that are exciting, inspiring, and joyous about medieval studies today, when you look at the current institutional landscape and job market results, it's hard to argue against the idea that our field is a community of very smart people doing interesting and important work...but mostly all by ourselves, with hardly anyone else outside that community paying attention to us. Almost every single medievalist I've ever known has reported feeling the same sense of melancholic dread I saw in Sad Ovid...and for good reason.

So, what can we do about it? This is probably the most important question facing the field today, but it's also (as such questions tend to be) extremely difficult to answer. Part of the reason for that is that there are many external social, economic, and political factors contributing to the crisis in medieval studies and the humanities in general. That includes things like the monetization of higher education, social inequalities, systemic racism, the politically-motivated scepticism and villainization of universities and academic expertise, and the prioritization of STEM fields at the expense of the humanities in primary and secondary education, among others. None of those problems can be solved by medievalists alone, which makes it difficult for any of us to see a way out of our current predicament.

---

2 Eisenberg with Kurtz, *Executive Summary of Medieval Studies Academic-Positions Update*.

The situation has understandably led to a profound sense of resignation in the field these days, one that has turned a great many medievalists into Sad Ovid, doing great work while staring longingly out the metaphorical window. My most visceral experience of this came at an academic gathering some years back, where I happened to overhear a medievalist professor at a major research university talking about how their program would not be accepting any new graduate students the following year. This was objectively bad news, yet, to my complete shock, this professional medievalist admitted feeling *relieved*, because they doubted they would be able to "find jobs" for all the graduate students already in their program, so it was probably good not to be getting any new ones. I seemed to be the only one struck dumb by that reaction; the other medievalists (most of them professors as well) standing nearby just shrugged or nodded knowingly. I found this incident profoundly depressing; the very people charged with leading the field into the future by training and developing future generations of medievalists seemed to agree that there was nothing to be done about this terrible predicament other than to sigh deeply and grimly press on with our work. Years later, that mentality was what I recognized in Sad Ovid's face.

The task before us all is clear: if our field is going to survive and thrive as we all hope, we need to leave our Sad Ovid days behind. Granted, the contributing factors to the crisis are systemic and complex, but the enormity of the task absolutely *cannot* be an excuse for us to sit idly and do nothing. Even if we can't solve every problem threatening our field on our own, we have to do *something*. I know I'm not the only one who feels this way; there are plenty of medievalists of all levels out there ready and willing to change things (and the fact that you're reading this book means you're probably one of them), and who are working very hard to solve it. But the challenge is so massive that it's hard even for these go-getters to feel like they're making any progress. That said, there are still plenty of other factors contributing to the precarious state of our field that we *can* change, so we should commit ourselves to working on improving as many of those factors as we can. Ideally, we would start by focusing on a particular issue that could, if we fixed it, make it easier to tackle the rest of the field's problems. And I think I know just where to begin.

In this book, I'm going to focus on a problem in medieval studies that I am convinced will go a long way towards ending our current crisis: public engagement. In my view, this issue is kind of like a through-line connecting all the other structural problems that have brought medieval studies to its precarious state. To put it another way, the main reason the field is losing institutional and material support so quickly is because too many people who aren't medievalists don't understand what the field does or why it's important. Therefore, in order to reverse that trend, the solution is for the field itself (i.e., all the professional medievalists and medievalists-in-training) to convince as many potential stakeholders as possible that expert knowledge about medieval culture is relevant, interesting, and, most importantly, *valuable*.

I wrote this book to help my fellow medievalists do exactly that. To be sure, it sounds simple enough, but practicing more effective public engagement will take a lot of work. As I'll explain in more detail below, our success depends on mastering a skill set that the current academic system isn't designed to teach. So to learn those necessary skills, medievalists will need to look elsewhere, specifically at a different intellectual culture where those skills were both highly valued and diligently taught. Fortunately, medievalists already know just such a system quite well: the intellectual culture of the European Middle Ages. It's here, right in the very subject matter at the core of the field, that we can find useful examples of professional intellectuals employing mindsets, practices, and tools to make their expertise understandable, engaging, and relevant to audiences well beyond their intellectual peers. In short, the key for medieval studies to set itself on course for a more promising future lies in the medieval past, just waiting for us to use it.

My Public Engagement Profile

I think the graduate school version of me would have been quite surprised to learn that public engagement beyond academia is now the main focus of my professional life. That's because my 2015 self could not have known that I would end up working at the Newberry Library in Chicago. I certainly was familiar with the Newberry back then, thanks to its rich collections of medieval manuscripts, printed books, and other objects. But in 2016, I was fortunate enough to be hired there as a Mellon Major Projects Fellow who was charged with coordinating a project entitled "Religious Change, 1450–1700." It was only then that I was really able to appreciate the quality that makes the Newberry truly special: unlike other institutions with similar collections, the Newberry is a *public* research library that has been free and open to anyone and everyone since 1887.[3] That public-facing orientation is at the core of the Newberry's institutional identity,

3 Spadafora, ed., *The Newberry 125: Stories from Our Collection*.

and everything that happens there, from public programs and events to research and instruction, is done with a broad range of potential publics (i.e., not just scholars) in mind.

The public character of the Newberry has informed all the work that I've done there, from my days as a postdoc trying to convince non-scholarly audiences to engage with our early modern religious collections to my current role in the Center for Renaissance Studies (CRS), in which my main job is to create programming and outreach initiatives that promote the knowledge and use our medieval and early modern materials. Altogether, I've spent my eight years at the Newberry developing and applying a set of skills, practices, and mindsets that have successfully made very old and esoteric books, art, and other objects understandable, interesting, and meaningful to all sorts of audiences...many of whom are not academics or students. I did all that through a laundry list of projects, initiatives, and activities that I had never even *imagined* doing in graduate school: curating multiple gallery exhibitions, developing digital resources, planning marketing campaigns, talking to the media, organizing public programs, designing pedagogical resources for high school classrooms, leading collection presentations, and much more besides.

In short, my time at the Newberry has given me a thorough and intensive training in how *not* to be Sad Ovid. Thanks to the Newberry's public-facing identity, I haven't had the opportunity to sit alone at my table full of books and sadly wonder why no one else is there. Instead, I've had to (metaphorically speaking) get up, get out, and *find* other audiences so I could convince them to care about the Middle Ages. Alongside all that practical experience, though, the Newberry has also given me a very different perspective on my work as a medievalist than the one I had in graduate school. Coming to the Newberry meant stepping outside of academia proper, which gradually allowed me to look back at medieval studies with new eyes. And as I've spent more and more time and effort engaging audiences beyond academia, those eyes have become much more critically aware of all the practices, mentalities, and assumptions that really only make sense within the academic system, but don't work nearly as well anywhere else. In short, it was through my Newberry eyes, if you will, that I was able to recognize medieval studies' public engagement problem.

The Public Engagement Problem in Medieval Studies

So, how exactly is public engagement a problem for medieval studies? Let's start with the basics. There are some pretty technical definitions of "public engagement" out there,[4] but for me, it's a pretty simple concept. I define it this way: **making a productive connection with some kind of audience.** I consider a "productive connection" to be one that convinces an audience (or audiences) to take some kind of action that accomplishes something that you want. That "something" could be just about anything: signing a petition, buying a product or service, liking and subscribing on social media, believing a point of doctrine, following rules and regulations, voting for a particular candidate, learning a skill, rectifying an injustice, understanding something about medieval culture, you name it. Whatever your goal, "public engagement" is the set of tools you use to get some kind of audience to think/believe/do what you want. These tools—which, in and of themselves, are neutral—could be just about anything that has ever been represented or expressed in any kind of medium: visual art, public speaking, private conversation, books, poetry, videos, social media, music, and so on. Anyone who is able to master these tools can convince an endless variety of audiences to think and do whatever is necessary to accomplish a particular goal.

This basic definition of public engagement applies to anyone, but I would add a bit more detail for the public engagement medievalists do: **making a productive connection between their expertise about the Middle Ages and some kind of audience(s).** This, on the surface, should not be anything new to medievalists. After all, they have been building productive connections with certain types of audiences extremely well for a very long time. These include, for example, professional academics (especially other medievalists) through things like scholarly monographs, articles and book chapters, lectures, and the like. Medievalists use these tools to convince other scholars to, among other things, learn new information about the Middle Ages, pursue new questions and avenues of research, and develop new approaches to teaching the Middle Ages. Another important audience medievalists engage extremely well is undergraduate students; from liberal arts colleges to R1 universities, medievalists are constantly developing assignments, active-learning exercises, lectures, PowerPoint presentations, and other pedagogical tools that successfully convince their students to understand, analyze, and get excited about the Middle Ages (for at least an academic term).

4 Frewer, "A Typology of Public Engagement Mechanisms."

The field's public engagement problem doesn't have anything to do with these audiences. Instead, it becomes obvious when we look beyond the university context (in which medievalists do most of their public engagement work) to how medieval studies engages audiences *outside academia.* When it comes to this sort of public engagement—and I'm going to be perfectly frank here—professional medievalists have been pretty ineffective, and that is why the field is in such dire straits. The proof is right there in the bare facts of our institutional crisis. Medievalists have been producing excellent scholarly publications and teaching engaging undergraduate courses for many decades now, yet the field continues to wither away before our eyes. That is because the forms of public engagement that medievalists have always done well are, relatively speaking, extremely limited in their impact. Scholarly publications, as we'll see a bit later, are not very accessible to audiences outside the field, and most undergraduates who enjoy medieval courses typically don't have much reason (or opportunity) to think about the Middle Ages after the grades are in.

Since neither of the traditional forms of public engagement medievalists practice effectively reaches audiences outside academic settings, it should come as no surprise that most people who aren't professional medievalists (or are on their way to becoming one) tend to see medieval studies as something like this: a niche scholarly field in which highly-trained academics with a lot of specialized skills use big words to talk to each other about the strange things people did a very long time ago (depending on where you live, you could also add "in a place very far away" to this, too).

In short, audiences outside academia tend to see medieval studies as *irrelevant,* and this leads to even bigger problems. After all, if what professional medievalists do doesn't really matter to anyone else, why bother making sure they have enough institutional or financial support? It would be far better for administrators and funders to spend their time, effort, and resources on things that make a positive contribution to everyone's lives, right? I'm sure this sounds very familiar to many medievalists out there. After all, this (or something very much like it) is the explanation we often hear from university administrators when they eliminate faculty positions in medieval studies, from grant review committees when they decline to invest money in medieval studies, and from parents who encourage their college-age children to major in something more financially secure.

But here's the thing that gets me the most about this. The common perception of the irrelevance of medieval studies stands in pretty stark contrast to the very real, widespread, and enthusiastic popularity of the Middle Ages themselves. As has been noted many times over, you can find representations or adaptations of medieval culture showing up everywhere in popular culture: literature, toys, children's books, games, movies and television shows, amusement parks, fan conventions, and more.[5] All these manifestations are proof that people without PhDs in medieval studies are not only interested in and excited about medieval things, they're also—and I can't emphasize this enough—*willing to spend time and money on them*. How, then, could a field built around understanding something so lucrative and popular be in such trouble?

It's clear to me that the Middle Ages themselves are not the cause of the field's irrelevance problem: we are. Or, to be more precise (and fair), the problem is *how professional medievalists share their expertise with non-medievalists*. If medieval studies appears esoteric and irrelevant to modern society—and the facts are pretty clear that it does—then it follows that medievalists must, at least in part, be presenting it that way, and probably have been for a long time. It's only in the past decade or so that the field as a whole has made it a stated priority to build productive connections with audiences outside of academia, so it shouldn't really be a surprise that those audiences still need a lot of convincing that our work matters. As if that weren't enough, in this time of crisis, far too many medievalists are still taking the Sad Ovid approach, morosely forging along with their scholarship and teaching with the faint hope that someone might suddenly notice that this work is interesting, important, and worth supporting. In my view, this disengaged approach has not only contributed to our institutional decline, it's also caused real harm in the world by making it easier for white supremacist groups to use medieval culture to support their racist, violent agendas without, until very recently, much pushback from those in the field.[6] In my view, it's hardly an overstatement to say that our public engagement problem could be the root of the entire crisis we're facing.

Therefore, I am convinced that, if we want to find our way out of our current predicament, we need to learn how to do more effective public engagement outside the academy. If we as a field can, unlike Sad Ovid, successfully build productive connections with diverse audiences beyond the university, we'll then be able to convince all kinds of stakeholders that our field is relevant, useful, and, perhaps most importantly, *essential* to modern society. And if we can do that, we will suddenly find it a lot easier to direct peoples'

5 Grollemond and Keene, *The Fantasy of the Middle Ages*.

6 Kim, "Teaching the Middle Ages in a Time of White Supremacy," and Lomuto, "White Nationalism and the Ethics of Medieval Studies."

interest, excitement, and financial support for medieval *things* into medieval *studies*. And once we do *that*, every other systemic problem threatening the field—lack of jobs, lack of students, lack of attention, etc.—becomes much, much easier to solve.

The good news is that this work is already being done. Advocacy and outreach have been major emphases for professional organizations like the Medieval Academy of America for some years now, and plenty of individual medievalists have been doing excellent work sharing their expertise in a lot of innovative and exciting ways. Some of my favourite examples (and this is a very small list) of this work includes books written for popular presses instead of academic ones (such as Christopher de Hamel's *Meetings with Remarkable Manuscripts*), colouring books (like Dayanna Knight's *The Viking Coloring Book*), comics (anything by Kristen Haas Curtis, but especially her adaptation of the *Nun's Priest's Tale*), children's books (my kids' favourite is Katy Beebe and S.D. Schindler's *Brother Hugo and the Bear*), "medieval" covers of popular songs (by YouTube artists like Hildegard von Blingin' or Algal the Bard), humorous videos on TikTok (#medievaltiktok and #medieval), novels (so many to choose from, but I particularly recommend Lucy Pick's *Pilgrimage*), and video and computer games (Ubisoft's *Assassin's Creed* series in particular). On top of all this, more and more senior and junior medievalists are serving as consultants on television shows and movies, making guest appearances on popular podcasts, and sharing content on social media. Better yet, even more medievalists than these are using these more effective public engagement techniques all the time in their teaching, so that they can spark the interest and curiosity of their students, many of whom step into the classroom without any pre-existing interest in the Middle Ages. All in all, it is fair to say that more professional medievalists today are attempting to engage audiences outside academia than ever before.

That's the good news...the bad news is that this terrific work isn't doing enough to end the crisis. No question, all this outreach should give every medievalist hope that it's possible for medieval studies to build productive connections with audiences outside academia, but we need more. In particular, we need *every* medievalist to be willing and able to make a *sustained* commitment to doing some kind of public engagement work beyond research and teaching. What's more, we also need all those medievalists to level up that public engagement from just making the Middle Ages interesting and accessible (which all of the work I mentioned above does) to using their expertise to make some kind of positive, measurable impact on our world today. That is, we as a field need to make it a priority to convince people that medieval studies can help develop solutions to social and economic inequalities, address health emergencies, shape legislation and political policies, create profitable business models, and so on.

Right now, the field is willing to do that kind of work, but it doesn't quite know how. And that is so because, at the macro level, public engagement beyond academia is still not a central enough priority for the field. For most medievalists (especially those at R1 universities), it's something *extra*. After all, reaching out to non-scholarly audiences is not the sort of thing that will get you tenure; when it comes to medievalists' professional lives, scholarship and teaching still reign supreme. And, really, that's not surprising at all. This situation is simply the natural product of the academic system in which all medievalists receive their professional development. That system has been designed to produce scholars and teachers, and that's exactly what it does. It has been that way pretty much since the nineteenth century, when medieval studies was transformed into a "scientific" field that could only be populated by experts (most of whom were privileged, white, and male).[7] Anyone who didn't approach medieval culture as "professionally" as that lot did, was deliberately belittled, criticized, and, crucially for our purposes here, ignored.

Our public engagement problem is the direct result of that fateful shift. The academic system that came out of that period was designed to train people to do their work within that system, either as a researcher or a teacher. As such, every medievalist I've ever known has left their doctoral training with a clear understanding of how to do research and how to teach a class, but not a single one of them has left having learned how to build productive connections with audiences outside the academy. Medievalists who *can* do this work either entered their program already knowing how to do it, or learned to do it completely on their own, in most cases without any support from their department. Left to itself, then, the academic system will, more often than not, keep on producing more professional medievalists who don't know how to convince the rest of the world that their work is valuable.

So, again, what are we going to do about this? To be clear, I don't believe the answer is to make that one great argument, write that one great op-ed article, or give that one great TED talk (all of which are just *slightly* more accessible versions of traditional academic public engagement anyway) that will go viral and convince everyone that the professional study of the Middle Ages matters. If we are going to solve this problem, we are going to need to

---

7 Gabriele and Whitaker, eds., "The Ghosts of the Nineteenth Century and the Future of Medieval Studies."

change the system. In particular, we need to change it so that it naturally produces medievalists who can engage audiences beyond academia just as well as they can research and teach.

But of course, there's another problem here: systemic change on this scale is hard, tends to take a long time (time the field may not have), and can be very scary, especially when the system has been around for as long as modern academia has. But make no mistake, we need to do something to bring about this change, and we need to start doing it *right now*, ideally by finding a way to make it easier for medievalists to develop and utilize effective public engagement skills alongside teaching and research skills. That alone, I think, would be enough to equip current and future generations of the field to make even more changes that will turn the steady decline of medieval studies around. But how exactly can we do that?

I think the best way to start this critical project is by thinking outside the box, namely, by bringing in some ideas, mindsets, and practices that are not so tied into the old system. And, come to think of it, it sure would help if we had some good models—that is, clear examples of habits, practices, and strategies that other people have used to build productive connections with various non-specialist audiences—to work with. When, where, and how have we seen a different way of doing things? Are there any examples of a professional development system that successfully produced individuals who had expert-level command of public engagement, rigorous academic inquiry, and teaching? As a matter of fact, there are plenty of them. Even better for medievalists, some of the very best of these models have been, as it were, right in front us this whole time, in the very medieval culture we study.

The Solution: Public Engagement in Medieval Europe

Perhaps you're wondering what medieval Europeans could possibly offer us to help solve the crisis of the humanities. I mean, how could people who could hardly have imagined our advanced communication technology and global culture possibly teach us anything about doing effective public engagement today? As I see it, professional intellectuals in the European Middle Ages—which I define as anyone who made their living off highly-specialized intellectual training in schools or universities (e.g., university professors, preachers, artists, clerics, ecclesiastical and secular administrators)—had a lot in common with professional scholars now. Like us, these individuals made their living by reading, researching, writing, and teaching; spent years studying and training to be considered experts in their fields; and usually worked alongside other elite scholars at major institutions.

However, we don't have to look very hard to see that, when it comes to public engagement with audiences outside the educated elite, we could hardly be more different from our forebears in medieval Europe. And no, this has nothing to do with a lack of technology. Unlike most scholars today, professional intellectuals in the European Middle Ages were *expected* to be really good at building productive connections with diverse audiences... especially those without advanced university degrees. To put it another way, if we wanted to visualize *their* field, we would not see Sad Ovid. Instead, we would see something much more like this book's cover image, in which St. John of Patmos is out and about in the world, preaching confidently to a group of laypeople (that included both men and women, no less) rather than sitting sadly alone in a room. The roots of the more proactive and public-facing intellectual culture of medieval Europe ran deep. Already in the fifth century, Augustine of Hippo had declared that any Christian intellectual "must communicate what is good and eradicate what is bad, and...must win over the antagonistic, rouse the apathetic, and make clear to those who are not conversant with the matter under discussion what they should expect."[8] Augustine's successors in medieval Europe took this lesson to heart; they understood that being a professional intellectual also meant that they had to be able to make their work understandable to *any* audience that was "not conversant with the matter," so that this new knowledge could convince them to change their lives.

This may seem extreme to professional humanities scholars today, but intellectuals in the Middle Ages could hardly have thought otherwise. In stark contrast to contemporary medievalists, their professional development system was set up to prepare them to build productive connections with audiences outside of the intellectual elite. This was due mostly to two of the most important pillars of medieval higher education: the liberal arts and Christianity. Inherited from classical intellectual culture, the liberal arts were intended to supply students with everything they needed to become responsible, discerning citizens. These same arts became the essential building blocks of medieval intellectuals' expertise, but none were more important than the three arts of the Trivium: grammar, rhetoric, and dialectic. It was from these subjects that medieval intellectuals learned how to use language (grammar), how to speak persuasively (rhetoric), and how to win arguments (dialectic). Rhetoric is probably the most important of these arts for understanding medieval public engagement, since it was this subject

8 Augustine, *On Christian Teaching*, trans. Green, bk. 4, chap. 4, 103.

that taught one how to express themselves convincingly.[9] It was mastering rhetoric that allowed intellectuals to make a real difference in the world, because they could use it to convince their contemporaries to think or do certain things they wanted.[10]

Christianity, the second pillar of medieval public engagement training, was probably the most powerful cultural force of all in medieval Europe. Most everyone, regardless of their place in society, lived in a world that revolved around Christian ideas, practices, and habits. For intellectuals, the connection was even stronger; most of them were trained and later employed within the structure of the church, so their work was expected to align with the main goals of institutional Christianity. Considering that most intellectuals were expected to not just read but *memorize* the entire Bible, they could hardly have missed that public engagement had been one of those institutional goals since the beginning: "Therefore go and make disciples of all nations," Christ himself had said, "baptizing them in the name of the Father and of the Son and of the Holy Spirit, and *teaching them to obey everything I have commanded you*" (Matthew 28: 19–20, my emphasis). In turn, the intellectual system that developed in Europe after the fall of the Roman Empire was designed to carry out that very mission. As such, any medieval intellectual who worked for the church (which was most of them) was expected to use their work to reach and convince any potential audience to do/think/believe something, whether it was full of experts or not.

The upshot of all this is that professional intellectuals in the Middle Ages finished their professional development equipped with two things medievalists today lack: 1) a set of highly-developed public communication skills and 2) a sense of obligation to use those skills to a make a difference in the world. Of course, then, as now, some professional intellectuals were better at (or more committed to) public engagement than others. The key difference is that, in medieval Europe, a commitment to public engagement beyond the academy was part of the job of being an intellectual. Unlike the elitist post-Enlightenment medievalists who ruled the roost in the nineteenth century, you'd have to look pretty hard to find a prominent medieval intellectual who *wasn't* working to engage audiences outside the professional elite in some way. This explains why we see an experimental monastic thinker like Anselm of Bec *also* putting together a set of prayers for a noblewoman;[11]

9 McKeon, "Rhetoric in the Middle Ages."

10 Cicero, *De inventione*, ed. Greco, 74.

11 See Anselm, *The Prayers and Meditations of St. Anselm with the Proslogion*.

elite university theologians *also* ministering to groups of spiritual women in cities like Paris;[12] scholastic titans like Albert the Great *also* showing up in popular legends and devotional works (even though they left no vernacular writings);[13] highly-skilled artisans and designers *also* putting mundane yet popular things like pretzels in expensive stained-glass windows in German churches;[14] and top-notch scholars like Jean Gerson *also* spending a lot of time writing vernacular versions of their more sophisticated Latin works to reach a wider readership.[15]

For medievalists keen on learning how to do better public engagement, this is *great* news. Because medieval intellectuals internalized effective public engagement strategies so well, we can find traces of those strategies in everything those intellectuals did. That means that all the texts, images, objects, ideas, and so on that they produced (or helped to produce) are a treasure trove of strategies, habits, tricks, hacks, and cautionary tales for how someone can successfully build productive connections with all kinds of non-expert audiences. In other words, all the helpful public engagement tools we modern medievalists could possibly want to use are right there in the very primary sources that are literally the foundation for our field. All we have to do is find a way to understand what those tools were and how they worked, so that we can pick them up and start using them today for ourselves. And that is what I hope this book will do.

What This Book Is

This book, as you've probably already noticed, is not your typical study of the European Middle Ages. In fact, I wouldn't call it "study" at all. I prefer to think of it as a *manual*, that is, a practical guide for you to learn how to do something. That "something" is this: **how to develop effective public engagement skills by adapting the medieval public engagement tools (i.e., practices, mindsets, and habits) you find in your sources**. In the rest of this book, I will explain how to do that by laying out what are, in my opinion, the very best practices of public engagement in the European Middle Ages. I'll talk about what those practices are, explain how they worked, and

12 See Miller, *The Beguines of Medieval Paris.*

13 See Gottschall, "Albert's Contributions to or Influence on Vernacular Literatures."

14 Cf. *Das Freiburger Münster* and Boivin, *Riemenschneider in Rothenburg.*

15 Hobbins, *Authorship and Publicity Before Print.*

offer suggestions, based on my own experience after I left graduate school, on how you can apply them now.

The advice I've gathered here can help medievalists of any level learn how to do better public engagement, from first-year graduate students to independent scholars to fully tenured professors. For those at an earlier stage in their career, this book will help you understand the importance of practicing good public engagement from the beginning of your professional development. For those who are more advanced, it can help you rethink how you think and talk about your expertise, and learn how to provide the necessary support for younger generations of medievalists to do the same.[16] Importantly, you don't need any particular background knowledge or ready-made skills to do this; this book focuses on the intellectual culture in medieval Europe because that's the aspect of the Middle Ages I know best, so it's where I can see these solutions most clearly. But at the same time, I firmly believe that the medieval public engagement tools I talk about (and plenty more besides) can be found in every subfield and discipline that make up medieval studies, so the model you'll find here will benefit you no matter what you study, whether it's the Islamic world, Mediterranean cultures, the global Middle Ages, or anything else.

More than that, I'm confident this book can be helpful for scholars and students in *other* humanities fields, as well. Though you may not study medieval sources, the strategies and approaches you'll find here should work just as well for other fields and disciplines. After all, the professional medieval intellectuals you'll meet shortly certainly didn't observe the same disciplinary or chronological boundaries that we fret over today, so there is no reason why their example can't work for other areas of study. Whoever you are and whatever you do, this book can prepare you to explain why your work is interesting, important, and valuable to the outside stakeholders (consumers, employers, administrators, institutions, funders, etc.) whose support we need to get us out of this crisis.

How This Book Works

I'm going to do all of this in five chapters. Four of these chapters are fairly brief case studies that tackle what I call "structural roadblocks": four practices or mindsets internalized by medievalists during our professional training that create the field's public engagement problem. Some of these are explicitly taught or encouraged by mentors in graduate school, but more

16 See also Cassuto, *The Graduate School Mess.*

often, we learn them implicitly by observing how all the medievalists around us do what they do. And, because we internalize these roadblocks in this way, we rarely ever notice them, much less think about them critically. As you'll see throughout the book, I repeatedly slammed face-first in to all four of them throughout graduate school and my brief adjuncting life. It was only when I stepped out of academia by coming to the Newberry that I was able to see them and recognize the damage they were doing. Because these roadblocks are hard to see from within the field, I will be talking about them in a pretty general and polemical way in the following chapters. I'm doing that to make them clearly visible, although I wouldn't blame you if it seemed like I'm building reductive strawmen to knock down. There are, as you'll see, perfectly understandable reasons why those roadblocks have developed, and I certainly do not mean to suggest that you or anyone else is a bad medievalist for practicing them, intentionally or not. But all the same, those roadblocks are, I'm quite certain, harming medieval studies, so I hope this book will help you learn to see them clearly so you can avoid them.

In this book, I take on the four structural roadblocks that I think are most responsible for medieval studies' public engagement woes. Chapter 1 deals with what I call the Life of the Mind Excuse, which refers to medievalists' default tendency to explain the value of their work only in terms of its impact on the field itself. Chapter 2 then takes on Genre Dependency, a term I use to describe the fact that medievalists are conditioned to prioritize sharing their knowledge about the Middle Ages in a scholarly publication. Chapter 3 turns to the General Public Fallacy, my term for an overly simplified understanding of non-academic audiences that short-circuits a lot of outreach initiatives before they start. Finally, chapter 4 sets its sights on Gatekeeping, which I take to mean the field's assumption that the true work of medieval studies—experiencing, interpreting, and talking about medieval culture (that is, the stuff that makes the field cool)— can *only* be done in the academy.

But fear not! Each case study also presents a medieval "solution" to the structural roadblocks and all the problems they cause. Every chapter is centred on a single medieval author or creator whose work shows those solutions in action especially well. Respectively, they are Peter Damian, Hildegard of Bingen, Henry Suso, and the anonymous compiler of a fifteenth-century devotional manuscript. In my view, these creators are the clearest examples of the habits, mindsets, and practices that medievalists should adopt if we want to build the productive connections with other audiences that we so desperately need. I would argue that they were all in force throughout the entire medieval period, but these examples all come from the western part of the European continent (mostly the German-speaking lands, as it turns out) in the period between approximately 1000 and 1500. I'm positive there are other authors or examples out there that are just as clear and compelling as the ones I've marshalled here; I believe these solutions could be found in any medieval intellectual's work, but these are the particular authors who made these solutions visible for me.

Chapter 1 starts with what I think is really the cornerstone of the whole thing, the Life of Service Conviction, which refers to elite medieval intellectuals' assumption that the whole point of their expertise was to have some kind of impact on the lives of *all* their contemporaries, not just their fellow intellectuals. Chapter 2 then brings in Genre Diversity, or, intellectuals' determination to prioritize multiple creative ways to share their expert knowledge that would make it more accessible to diverse audiences. Next, chapter 3 talks about Audience Development, the lengthy, intensive, yet ultimately effective process elite intellectuals used to cultivate receptive audiences for their work. Finally, chapter 4 focuses on Audience Empowerment, which I think of as the whole endgame of public engagement in medieval Europe: training and inviting non-experts of all kinds, including laypeople (i.e., non-academics), to participate actively in the work of elite intellectual culture.

Following those case studies is a final chapter that I'm calling a "game plan" instead of a traditional conclusion. If chapters 1–4 are about laying the groundwork for a medieval model of effective public engagement, chapter 5 is about how you can implement that model in your own work. As you'll see, I think the key to the whole thing is as simple as thinking intentionally about public engagement, identifying the tools that can help you achieve it, and diligently practicing using those tools as much as possible. So, to help you do that, this final chapter goes over some simple activities that you can practice while you're doing your thing as a medievalist—taking courses, preparing for comprehensive exams, designing and teaching courses, researching in the archives, or writing a monograph or dissertation—that will set you up for public engagement success later. Along the way, you'll also hear quite a bit about me and my experiences in graduate school, adjuncting and, most importantly, my time doing public outreach at the Newberry Library, where I've seen every one of these medieval solutions in action, which gives me confidence that they can work for you, too.

* * *

I wrote this book because I love medieval studies, and I want the field not just to survive the current crisis, but to thrive for generations to come. To do that, it needs to change. Going forward, medieval studies need to become more open and accessible, more global, more diverse and antiracist, more compassionate and accommodating, and more flexible and creative. We've made some progress in all these areas, but there is a long way to go.[17] Making effective public engagement more central to the field and its training is a way to make all this change happen (and happen more quickly), so I wrote this book to help make that a reality. But I also wanted to do that with a book that *only a medievalist could write*. That's why you'll still find me analyzing primary sources, citing secondary literature, translating texts from their original languages, and discussing the cultural context of the European Middle Ages. I want you to see how a professional medievalist (for that's how I think of myself) can use their expertise today to offer practical solutions to a contemporary problem. Indeed, everything you see me do in this book is ultimately rooted in the knowledge I gained through years of researching why religious thinkers wrote so many letters in the eleventh and twelfth centuries. I'm sure your content expertise, whatever it may be, can accomplish all sorts of useful things that will help address the many other crises and catastrophes out there. After all, the tools provided by our individualistic post-Enlightenment culture don't seem to be able to solve them, so we could use some different solutions, and the Middle Ages could be a great place to find them. I hope that this book will help open your eyes to all the good you can do as a medievalist right now, once you start to look at what you do and what you know from the right perspective. If we can all do that, I think we'll all be able to set medieval studies on course for a more secure future.

17 Otaño Gracia, "Welcome to a New Reality!"

Chapter 1

PETER DAMIAN AND THE LIFE OF SERVICE CONVICTION

The Problem: The Life of the Mind Excuse

"A degree in medieval studies? What are you going to do with that?" If you're reading this book, I'm going to assume that you've heard a version of this question at some point in your life...probably lots of times, and from lots of people. That's certainly been the case for me and pretty much everyone I know in the field, and I think it's safe to say that dealing with sceptical questions like these is just part of what being a medievalist means these days. Indeed, I wasn't a graduate student for very long before I noticed that swapping tales of family members, friends, or complete strangers asking us what we could possibly do with a degree in medieval studies was something of a team-building activity for graduate students huddled together at conference receptions.

I've taken part in many of those impromptu support sessions myself, and always found them comforting, because we all assured each other that following our hearts into this field that didn't seem to make sense to anyone else was the right decision. Looking back now, though, I can't help but notice something that my fellow graduate students and I usually *weren't* doing during all that team-building: actually answering those sceptical questions. The support was great, but it would have been better if we were also putting our heads together to come up with things we actually *could* do with our medieval expertise that would make a difference in peoples' lives. I don't blame myself or my fellow graduate students for not doing this; after all, why would we? Everyone present there already knew that medieval studies were important, so explaining its relevance today didn't seem necessary. What none of us realized—what none of us *could* have realized at the time—was that we had run smack into the first structural roadblock I want to talk about, the Life of the Mind Excuse.

I consider this roadblock to be the root of medieval studies' public engagement problem, because it heavily influences how medievalists tend to think about why their work is important. In this chapter, I'll explain how the default approach is designed to be received by other academics (and therefore, doesn't work well with anyone else), how that approach is the exact opposite of the way in which medieval intellectuals thought (and talked) about their expertise, and how I didn't realize that difference until I was quite unexpectedly using my own knowledge of medieval culture to do my day-to-day work at the Newberry.

To be clear, the life of the mind is not a bad thing. Seeking knowledge for knowledge's sake or loving learning are both great, and I know that they have led plenty of folks into medieval studies. What I'm talking about here is strictly a public engagement issue, and in that area, the "life of the mind" is, at least in my view, not all that helpful. If you need a good example of that, look no further than our good friend Sad Ovid. As Federica Caneparo explained to me, the viewers of this portrait were supposed to notice that the great poet wasn't *doing* anything with the books, tools, or anything else in his study; as she put it, "Everything that matters is in his head."

The Life of the Mind Excuse works the same way. That makes it problematic, to say the least, when people use "the life of the mind" to explain why something is important or worth supporting. Unfortunately, medievalists do this *all the time*. Think about it for a second, how have you answered the question "why are you doing medieval studies" in the past? Based on the conversations I've had with fellow medievalists over the years, I'm going to hazard a guess that you said something like "I think it's interesting," or "I really love it," or maybe "I want to understand it." In other words, what you do with medieval studies is all about some sort of personal or academic interest. Or, to put it another way, everything about the field that matters is in your own head.

If you've found yourself saying those things, you're in good company. In fact, all three of those quotes above are exactly how I explained why medieval studies mattered as a graduate student. And why wouldn't I? Everything in my training taught me that's how medievalists were *supposed* to talk about the importance of the particular knowledge they'd developed about the Middle Ages through their research and writing. If you want proof, go ahead and grab the nearest book or journal article from medieval studies and find the thesis statement. When you do, chances are you'll find a sentence that sounds a lot like this: "[this study] sheds light on the broader implications the widespread popularity letter-writing had for our understanding of the practice of religious thought and the formation and character of intellectual culture in the eleventh and twelfth centuries."[1] If you didn't stop to check the note, this is the thesis of my dissertation, that is, the sentence in which

1 Fletcher, "'Understand, Delight, and Obey,'" 1.

I tell the world why all the reading, thinking, transcribing, translating, and writing I had done in my six-ish years in graduate school *mattered*. And my answer was that it would help a relatively small group of experts know a little bit more about one aspect of a particular period of the medieval past than they did before. This is what the Life of the Mind Excuse looks like, and it is certainly not the kind of thing that would get someone outside of academia excited, interested, and invested in my work.

That's why I see this roadblock as the root of the weed currently choking effective public engagement in medieval studies. Thanks to the Life of the Mind Excuse, professional medievalists have been trained to explain the value of their expertise in terms of what it can do *for other professional medievalists*, which does not often translate well to other audiences. This is not to say, of course, that every professional medievalist shies away from explaining the value of their work to a non-specialist audience; many can do it quite well, but they tend to be pretty well established professionally by the time that they can. As mentioned earlier, very few graduate students are encouraged to explain the value of their work outside of an academic context; instead, most of them are told to focus on their dissertations, the value of which they tend to express in jargony thesis statements like mine. Later on, when graduate students are finally urged to start explaining why their work matters, the "elevator pitches" they come up with are aimed at search committees for academic jobs. With the system set up in this way, it's no wonder that, even though many medievalists are eventually able to talk about their work in a more engaging and open way, many more never do.

So, before we can talk about any other tactic for improving medievalists' public engagement efforts, we need to uproot the Life of the Mind Excuse. This doesn't mean that we should stop learning for the sake of learning or participating in scholarly conversations, but it *does* mean we should make articulating how our field impacts the world outside academia more central to what medieval studies is all about. If we do that, then we need no longer fear questions about "what we're going to do" with our work, because everyone in the field will have been trained to have a compelling answer at hand. Right now, of course, that's not how the field is set up, so we'll have to look elsewhere for help figuring out how to do this. Conveniently enough, the intellectual culture of medieval Europe is a great place to start.

The Medieval Solution: The Life of Service Conviction

You probably already got an idea from the Introduction that professional medieval intellectuals did not sweat the Life of the Mind Excuse. For most of them, the idea that their expertise was only supposed to benefit their peers was as foreign to them as it is familiar to us. Pick pretty much any aspect of intellectual culture in the European Middle Ages, and you'll find someone talking about how it could make some impact far beyond the medieval university or monastic cloister. To name just a few, monks and nuns developed highly-structured and complex regimens of prayer and devotion inside the cloister so they could benefit the souls of people outside it; bishops, priors, and other social elites used their own conduct and lifestyles as ways for training effective secular and ecclesiastical administrators; university doctors of theology compiled dense doctrinal treatises so the church could effectively combat heresy in cities and villages throughout Latin Christendom; patrons, artists, artisans, and labourers collaborated (often anonymously) to create stunningly decorated spaces that instructed the unlearned at the same time as they displayed wealth and status. You get the idea. Simply put, medieval intellectuals took for granted that their work was supposed to make some kind of visible (and, in their minds, positive) impact in the lives of everyone else in Latin Christendom, because that's exactly what their training prepared them to do.

This didn't mean, of course, that professional scholars didn't find their work interesting, or that they didn't love learning, or that they believed everyone in their society could engage with their work on the same level as their peers could. Furthermore, I think it's probably true that not every intellectual was all that interested in making an impact in the world outside their cloister or classroom. But, thanks to their training and the general orientation of the culture in which they participated, most all of them would have had a clear sense of how their work could benefit everyone around them and, unlike too many medievalists today, would have been ready to explain how if they were asked (or, as was often the case, even if they weren't). In other words, instead of excuses, they had *conviction*. We need the latter if we want to get past the Life of the Mind Excuse, and medieval intellectuals can show us the way to develop it. In this chapter, we'll do this by looking at a particularly elite religious thinker who was the living embodiment of an intellectual career based on public service.

The Model: Peter Damian

Our first medieval model is Peter Damian (ca. 1007–1072), an influential reformer, administrator, and theologian. As far as intellectuals went in the eleventh century, he was as elite as they came: he was renowned throughout Europe for his prodigious learning, his mastery of a wide array of sources, his unparallelled rhetorical and pedagogical skills, and his prolific, acclaimed writings.[2] At least on paper, he had the kind of career that any academic today might give their eyeteeth to have. But interestingly, Damian himself was pretty clear that he wasn't interested in any of that stuff. Born to a large family of modest means in Ravenna, he didn't grow up intending to be a learned saint, and even started his career as a secular teacher. But, shortly before he turned thirty, a spiritual crisis convinced him to join the religious life. Finding Benedictine monasticism a bit too easy-going for his tastes, he joined the hermitage of Fonte Avellana on the eastern coast of Italy, eventually becoming prior in 1043. For the rest of his life, Damian insisted that all he wanted to do was spend every day in his cell, blissfully praying the Psalter and contemplating the mysteries of the divine. Public engagement of any kind seemed quite far from his mind.

Damian's actions, though, told a different story. As much as he loved his hermitage, he didn't end up spending much time there. Rather, his contemporaries were more likely to find him out on the move, putting his extensive learning to work in a variety of public-facing projects and initiatives. Indeed, it had been that way from the beginning. He had hardly set foot in Fonte Avellana when two consecutive archbishops and "many citizens of Ravenna" summoned him back home "to stay in the hopes of winning back the souls living there." Although some early setbacks prevented him from remaining there long, Damian did not simply go back to his cell. On the contrary, "driven by a zeal [to serve] my neighbours," he "wandered throughout many regions in Italy with clear purpose of mind to acquire as bountiful a harvest of souls as I could…while also going around to call others back onto the right path" (Ep. 8, 1:118–20).[3]

He wasn't alone. The mid-eleventh century was a time that saw a series of spiritual reform movements sweep through the Latin Church that were, generally speaking, committed to restoring the fallen world to the divine exem-

2 Blum, *St. Peter Damian*.

3 This chapter relies mainly on Kurt Reindel's four-volume MGH edition of Peter Damian's *Epistolae*. I will cite it using the letter number, volume of Reindel's edition, and page number (e.g., Ep. 1, 1:65).

plar by changing the thoughts and behaviours of everyone in Latin Christendom.[4] Damian, though, seems to have stood out from the other reformers in the Italian lands, and he was drafted into the intellectual circle surrounding Pope Leo IX to help instil reform throughout the institutional church. He did that so well that he was eventually (despite repeated protests) elevated to the cardinal bishop of Ostia in 1057. From then on, he worked tirelessly as a religious thinker, administrator, legislator, diplomat, and general fixer for the papacy. Along the way, he practiced just about every form of public engagement he could: preaching sermons, giving orations at councils and synods, arguing legal cases, debating opponents in person and in writing, and having personal conversations with anyone who would listen, whether they wanted to or not. In the end, his efforts made profound contributions to some of the most important intellectual and social developments of his time.[5]

In other words, Damian was an elite intellectual whose work made a clear impact on his world, and I think he has a lot to teach us about how we can do the same. The important thing for us here are Damian's means, not his goals, so should start with a close look at *how* he shared his expertise, which turns out to be pretty easy to do. Although Damian surely produced all manner of writings during his career, the vast majority of his work survives in just one format: an extensive collection of letters, the largest one by a single author since the Patristic era.[6] This was 100 per cent intentional; Damian worked carefully with a couple editors to make sure that the letters, like all such collections, left a comprehensive overview of interests, his style, his erudition, and his service to the church.[7] In other words, the letters were something like a visible record of how Damian had conducted his intellectual career, or, if you like, the "receipts" for how he used his expertise to make a difference in the world.

Thanks to all that careful curation, Damian's letters are ideal sources for understanding the role the Life of Service Conviction played in his intellectual life. In them, just as Damian intended, we see him bringing his expertise to all manner of Christians (from high-ranking prelates and secular rulers to novice monks and middling nobility) in a variety of ways. More importantly for us, we also see him—constantly and without any prompting—explaining why his expertise was valuable to all his various correspondents.

---

4 Constable, *The Reformation of the Twelfth Century.*

5 Cf. Blum, *St. Peter*, 13–36; and Ranft, *The Theology of Peter Damian*, 108–84.

6 Blum, *St. Peter*, 40.

7 Reindel, "Studien zur Überlieferung der Werke des Petrus Damiani."

What's more, he knew perfectly well how challenging this could be. Perhaps the best example of this came from Ep. 17, which was written to a nobleman identified in the letters only as T.[8] Whoever T. was, he was clearly not a highly-trained intellectual or a devout monk or hermit, so it made perfect sense for Damian to assume that T. was as sceptical of the value of Damian's expertise as most non-medievalists today are of medieval studies: "What, I ask you...," Damian imagined him saying, "can something that is useless for me to know possibly teach me?" (1:164). Faced with this challenge, however, Damian did not talk about transferable skills or scholarly conversations; he talked about how what he knew could change lives. Damian's letters give us the perfect model for seeing the Life of Service Conviction in action. In the next sections, we'll talk about how that mindset shaped the ways in which he understood and shared what he knew with others. If we can get a solid sense of *why* he wrote his letters at all, *what* he thought they really were, and *how* he structured them accordingly, we'll have a better understanding of what we need to do to get some conviction in our own work.

Why Damian Wrote

To hear him tell it, Peter Damian's decades-long letter-writing campaign was not something he actually wanted to do. He often claimed he was "forced" to write many of his letters, so much so that later scholars would describe him as a "compulsive" letter-writer who instinctively turned to the genre whenever he felt compelled to say or do something.[9] Even that term is underselling it a bit. Although many of Damian's letters were written in response to particular requests, plenty more were written when no one had asked for them, and Ep. 104 (an account of a prominent noblewoman's confession) probably never should have been written at all.[10] For our purposes in this book, though, this is great; Damian's inability to resist writing letters is what makes him such a great model for the Life of Service Conviction. Letters, you see, were far and away the most *active* written genre around in the eleventh century; they were widely understood to be much more persuasive than commentaries and treatises, so authors (especially reformers) liked to use them when they wanted to make someone else do or think something to further their goals.[11]

---

8 On T.'s possible identity, see Reindel, *Die Briefe des Petrus Damiani*, 1:155n1.

9 Cf. Blum, *Letters of Peter Damian*, 1:12, and Leclercq, *Saint Pierre Damien*, 151–52.

10 Blum, *Letters of Peter Damian*, 4:155n55.

11 Fletcher, "Rhetoric, Reform, and Christian Eloquence."

Damian obviously was a part of this trend, but in his case, there was something else driving his dependence on letter-writing: fear. This emotion was the engine that drove Damian's entire intellectual and spiritual career; everything from his pursuit of a strict form of asceticism to his zealous defence of the church from any impurity (as he understood it) was rooted in how terrified he was of being found wanting at the Last Judgment. In fact, it was this, as he called it, "beneficial fear" (*salubrem formidinem*) that compelled him to enter the religious life in the first place, since he could live an "upright life" much more easily in a hermit's cell than in the middle of the world's temptations (Ep. 21, 1:210). But, as we've already seen, that wasn't quite good enough. Even in the supposed safety of his hermitage, Damian was afraid. What about all those people who, for one reason or another, couldn't or wouldn't take religious vows? Who would help *them* get into heaven? What would God do if Damian never used his deep learning and rhetorical brilliance to teach the non-specialists what they needed to believe or do in order to be saved? He was afraid of the answer. "For if I should live unproductively," he reasoned in Ep. 8, written at an early crossroads in his career, "I am terrified that the Gospel axe will be set at the roots of my tree, about which the Truth frighteningly thunders, saying 'Cut it down, why should it stay in the ground?'" (1:120).

Damian's "beneficial fear" would not allow him to be content with just the Life of the Mind. Instead, it convinced him that he had a responsibility to use his prodigious intellectual gifts to help as many people as possible find salvation, and he made sure everybody knew it.[12] He often told his correspondents that he wrote his letters "not because they would be helpful for me, but so that you might benefit from my counsel" (Ep. 12, 1:130). At the same time, he expected his letters to make their recipients (or, indeed, anyone who read or heard them) productive, too. He once proudly referred to them as "nails and goads" (*clavis et stimulis*), instruments of persuasion that both clarified divine truths for others and inspired them to live a virtuous life that would guarantee salvation (Ep. 21, 1:203). Those extremely high stakes are right there in Ep. 1, which was addressed to his friend, Honestus of Pomposa, a layperson. Honestus, it seems, had asked the recently converted hermit to write him something to refute Jews who wanted to debate the validity of Christianity. Although Damian was not entirely convinced that the effort was necessary, he wrote the letter anyway "because this knowledge certainly pertains completely to the faith, and faith is without question

12 Fletcher, "'Understand, Delight, and Obey,'" 145–63.

the foundation of all virtues, and whenever the foundation is shaken, the destruction of the entire structure is seriously threatened" (1:65–66).

If it seems a bit extreme to you that not answering a friend's unnecessary request could lead to the downfall of Christianity, you're not alone. But this was the kind of power beneficial fear had in Damian's intellectual life. He clearly wanted his readers to feel it, too, considering the many times he told his correspondents they were doing something that would lead themselves or someone else to damnation. For example, he told monks who were too interested in secular affairs that their actions would cause any laypeople who saw them to lose hope in the possibility of their own salvation (Ep. 165, 4:186). Likewise, when Duke Godfrey of Tuscany focused too much on pursuing a life of monastic virtue instead of enforcing justice in his lands, Damian reminded him that he was "without doubt the devil's accomplice" for exposing so many innocents to unchecked violence and abuse (Ep. 67, 2:283). He even went so far as to "terrify" and "restrain" a nobleman and his wife from cutting his mother out of decision-making in his household, citing a litany of stories in which God dispensed divine wrath on those who disrespected their parents (Ep. 86, 2:458–59).

Damian himself recognized that this approach was a little much. He knew just how hyperbolic he could be while sharing his expertise, but he was convinced that it was worth it, no matter what anyone else thought. As he once explained to a friend in Ep. 19, "Someone may say that I have gone overboard with my words, but the salvation of my neighbour is so important to me that I do not think it silly to light an enormous fire in order to kill a tiny poisonous lizard if that were necessary to keep the people safe" (1:198). This sentence, perhaps better than any other, sums up why Damian wrote: he was afraid of what would happen—to himself and others—if he didn't.

What Damian Wrote

What, according to Damian, were his letters? The answer is a bit complicated; Damian, like many other letter-writers of his day, used a variety of names for these texts (*epistola, littera, brevis, opusculum*, and so on).[13] No one at the time would have been surprised by this; the medieval epistolary genre was, to put it mildly, infinitely flexible, and authors freely used it to create all kinds of texts that did all kinds of different things.[14] Damian took

13 Fletcher, "'Understand, Delight, and Obey,'" 24.

14 Van Engen, "Letters, Schools, and Written Culture," 106.

full advantage of that flexibility; Ep. 1 alone includes four different genres (scriptural commentary, dialogue, peroration, argument from reason), and the rest of the collection features almost every kind of prose genre imaginable in the eleventh century: exegetical commentaries, theological explications, hagiographies, anecdotes, chronicles, panegyrics, bestiaries, mock trials, and more.

But even with all that versatility, Damian was consistent about what he thought all his letters, whatever form they took, were supposed to do. For starters, he was adamant that each and every one was "useful" or "beneficial" to whomever read or heard it (Cf. Epp. 12, 80, 93, 105, and 133). He was so confident in this because, at the end of the day, all his letters were really about the same thing: "my grammar is Christ...and only whatever can be consulted for the edification (*aedificationi*) of my brothers in Christ is recognized to emit from my letter" (Ep. 21, 1:203). Accordingly, Damian never sent (or, at least, never preserved) a letter that did not have some kind of spiritual lesson, admonition, or explication in it. When it came to securing the "edification" of his fellow Christians, Damian used everything in his intellectual toolbox. That included all the content we would expect from a highly educated cleric in medieval Europe: citations from nearly every book of the Bible, commentaries, theological works, chronicles and histories, canon law, synodal and conciliar proceedings, letters, monastic rules, and so on. At the same time, he also used material that was more accessible to non-elite audiences, such as saints' lives, liturgical prayers, and even stories he'd heard in casual conversations with clerics and laypeople. All of this—that is, everything that Damian knew—provided the raw material for the "nails and goads" that put his reform agenda into practice.

That said, Damian did not necessarily *want* his recipients to think of his letters as something that changed how they thought or acted. This was a pretty big ask even in the eleventh century, so he preferred that his readers think of them as opportunities or, perhaps better, *invitations* for their own spiritual and intellectual development. He made this clear near the end of Ep. 21, when he addressed the copious biblical quotes he had included in the letter, reminding his correspondent that "I *lay out before you* not my own words, but examples from holy Scripture" (1:210, my emphasis). The verb Damian chose here is really important; unlike other words he could have used (like "cite" or "quote"), *proponere* invites some action from the reader, specifically, to pick up what had been laid before them in order, we assume, to then do something with it. Sometimes Damian felt compelled to spell that out, in case his correspondents missed the point, as he did to Honestus in Ep. 1: "Therefore you have everything necessary for a conflict of this sort set before your eyes. Use the material I have prepared for you however you think is best" (1:102).

Ep. 1 is not an isolated example. Whenever he included Scripture in a letter (which was basically all the time), Damian encouraged his recipients to actively engage with it. His citations often include commands— like "weigh carefully," "consider," "pay close attention," or "take note"—that functioned like directions showing his readers how to work through whatever he had cited. This was another reason why Damian liked to write letters; unlike a sermon or an in-person conversation, his readers could, theoretically, read his letters again later if they wanted or needed to.[15] Even more remarkably, Damian encouraged his readers—including laypeople—to use the Scripture he provided as a starting point for reading more of it *on their own*. For instance, when he offered some Bible quotes in Ep. 179 to console a distraught nobleman, he also encouraged him to seek out "other witnesses in holy Scripture" (*aliisque scripturae divinae testimoniis*) that would aid in his recovery (4:291).

Damian treated all the other elite intellectual material in his letters in exactly the same way, placing it before his readers and instructing them how to use it. For that reason, we should think of his letters as *resources* for edification; that is, well-sourced and carefully constructed collections of "useful" content that would clearly define what the "upright life" was, how to follow it, and why it was important to do so. Damian himself explicitly talked about his letters being used this way. For example, he recommended "the letter that I wrote to Countess Blanche" (Ep. 66) to two recipients asking about the Last Judgment, since he had dealt with the subject pretty comprehensively there (Epp. 92–93). When he wrote to Adelaide of Turin (Ep. 114) to enlist her help in ending clerical marriage in her territories, he assumed that she had also seen and read Ep. 112, which had been addressed to Cunibert, the bishop of Turin (3:296). He even expected the citizens of Florence, who were embroiled in a controversy over the validity of sacraments performed by unreformed clergy at the time, to have read Ep. 40, also known as the *Liber gratissimus*, one of Damian's longest and most theologically dense letters on any subject (Ep. 146, 3:533). In short, it's clear that he wanted his letters to not just poke and prod people into doing, thinking, or believing something, but to give them the information they needed to understand *why* they needed to do, think, or believe it.

---

15 Reindel, "Petrus Damiani und seine Korrespondenten," 217.

How Damian Wrote

Of course, saying your work is useful to anyone and actually *making* it useful to anyone are two very different things. This was true even in the eleventh century, so we should take a minute to appreciate how difficult this was to do, especially considering the astonishing range of audiences for whom Damian wrote. Far from just writing to other elite intellectuals, Damian's letters show him sharing his expertise with all levels of the spiritual and secular hierarchies: popes and emperors, prelates and prominent nobility, monks and secular city officials, and everything in between. That range only increases if we factor in the many in-person conversations Damian mentions in his letters, which show him debating and teaching secular scholars, large groups of citizens, and even devout peasants.

Quite a few modern scholars have argued that Damian couldn't possibly have been serious about effectively teaching such a diverse group of audiences, so he must have written mainly for his ecclesiastical colleagues, who, at the very least, could read Latin.[16] That argument makes sense on the surface. After all, it's striking how consistent the overall tone, source material, and basic rhetorical approaches are throughout every letter, whether it was addressed to an elite intellectual like Desiderius of Monte Cassino or an unknown layperson going through a difficult time.[17] He also made surprisingly little distinction in terms of content, freely recommending to laypeople the sorts of texts we might assume were more appropriate for highly-trained intellectuals. For instance, Damian confidently directed his sister to read Augustine's *City of God*, Jerome's *Explanation of the Prophet Daniel*, and the book of the Apocalypse along with its commentaries in order to understand the Last Judgment, the exact same reading list he recommended to a monk interested in the same subject (Ep. 93, 3:28).

However, while I won't deny that he probably considered other professional intellectuals his *primary* audience, I don't think that means he considered them his *only* audience. I rather doubt Damian would have been confident that "But they didn't know Latin!" would be a satisfactory excuse for not edifying the laity as much as he could on Judgement Day. Not only that, there is pretty substantial evidence to suggest that even Damian's lay correspondents would have been able to access the letters, either because they knew Latin themselves or had someone who could translate for them at

---

16 Cf. Blum, *St. Peter*, 72, and Leclercq, *Saint Pierre*, 67.

17 Ranft, *Theology*, 196.

court.[18] In any case, I think the more-or-less unified tone and approach we see across the letters is evidence for the opposite of what most scholars have assumed about Damian's audience; rather than seeing it as proof that he always wrote for his fellow elites, it helps us to think about how Damian tried to express his elite expertise in ways that would work for *non-expert* audiences as well. That might be the reason why, for example, he shared more accessible material like anecdotes, *exempla*, and other popular stories with his more erudite colleagues. The point of this unified style, in other words, was to make his letters into something that could engage anyone who read or heard its contents.

He learned how to do that not in the cell, but from his time as a secular liberal arts instructor in Ravenna, an experience that clearly influenced how he handled the rest of his career.[19] I think we can see the letters' style as part of an attempt to recreate the classroom setting; that is, the rhetorical approaches in the letters were meant to bring his audiences—wherever and whoever they might be—into a space where they could learn how to change their lives directly from Damian. Incidentally, this makes his example particularly useful for medievalists, who are also expected to make their expertise engaging and useful for uninitiated audiences (i.e., undergraduates) in the courses they teach. What Damian shows us, however, is how to keep that pedagogical magic going in places beyond the physical classroom.

One way he established his epistolary classroom was by recreating the in-person interaction between instructor and student, adopting a style that resembled living speech more than an inert text. This fit very well with the medieval epistolary genre; since all letters (even the boring ones) were customarily read aloud to their recipients by messengers, an element of oral performance was in the genre's DNA.[20] His correspondents certainly seemed to think that was the case; a young monk named Ambrose asked him to explain the basic tenets of Christianity in a letter because, Damian recalled, he "would be more effectively instructed, and this teaching would stick more tenaciously in [his] mind, if I *in my own voice* explained what is found in the writings of the ancient fathers" (Ep. 81, 2:417, my emphasis). Throughout the collection, Damian made sure to preserve as many traces of face-to-face engagement with his readers as he could. Sometimes this meant modulat-

18 Cf. Fletcher, "'Understand, Delight, and Obey,'" 151–55; Thompson, *Literacy of the Laity*; and Petrucci, *Writers and Readers*.

19 Little, "The Personal Development of Peter Damian," 327.

20 Hoffman, "Zur mittelalterlichen Brieftechnik."

ing the volume and tenor of his "voice," like when he tried to convince the former empress Agnes to return to her religious life in Rome in Ep. 149 by speaking "more quietly" instead of "with shouts" (3:551). At other times, Damian sharply admonished his reader by demanding "Are you listening to what I am saying?" as if their mind had wandered off while he gave his lesson (Ep. 104, 3:550). And when he had a *really* important point to make, Damian liked to ratchet up the emotional energy behind his words, emphasizing the intense anger, joy, terror, or fear behind whatever argument he was making. Putting it mildly, Damian could get very *dramatic* in his letters, like the time he "collapsed...pouring out tears" at the feet of Widger, bishop of Ravenna, in Ep. 7, asking for tax relief for an impoverished monastery (1:117).

Another way Damian maintained his epistolary classroom was by walking his "students" through whatever content he had to share, as if he were standing in the room with them. He knew perfectly well that his arguments often depended on interpreting dense theological material, so he always made sure his students had the scaffolding and sign-posting they needed to get through it. Like any good teacher, he did not throw them into the deep end, but encouraged them to "look first at simple things, and from these small things consider what is beyond comprehension." Take, for example, how he explained the tricky concept of Christ's virgin birth to the new monk Ambrose:

> To wit, a sunbeam comes through a glass window, passing completely through the obstacle through some imperceptible kind of elusiveness. Yet this does not affect the solidity of the glass in any way, which afterwards looks the same from the inside and outside. Moreover, the glass is not broken when the sunbeam first enters it nor when it passes through, but maintains its integrity through the beam's coming and going. Therefore, if a sunbeam does not shatter a piece of glass, cannot the divine nature of the redeemer also remain intact after being born from a virgin? (Ep. 81, 2:423–24).

This is clearly the approach of someone used to working with novices. In fact, the example he uses to bring Ambrose into this divine mystery is so simple that it would have resonated with anyone who had ever seen a window before...perhaps even with people who weren't monks, clerics, or scholars.

He did the same thing with the abundance of Scripture quotations in his letters, which could be the most difficult source his lay readers (who were definitely *not* experienced exegetes) encountered. Mindful of that, he always offered his own interpretation to get them started, sometimes encouraging his readers to actually see themselves in it. That's what Adelaide of Turin found in Damian's explanation of Judges 4:5, in which he compares her to the Israelite judge Deborah:

> And just in the same way, you also rule your territory without the help of a man, and people with lawsuits and legal cases come to you from all over, seeking your judgment. But take note, that just like her you also rest under a palm tree between Ramah and Bethel. Ramah, indeed, is taken to mean "the highest," while Bethel means "the house of the Lord." Therefore, always sit under this same palm tree contemplating the victory of the cross of Christ standing above you (Ep. 114, 3:297).

Additionally, Damian was always aware of his students' limitations, and he avoided giving them more than they could handle. This might seem a bit odd to modern eyes, considering how densely packed the letters are with Scriptural, theological, and rhetorical content, but he insisted that they included only the bare minimum that was necessary for his readers to understand his point. Even in his longest letters, Damian always liked to remind everyone that he could have included even *more* content. In a letter to one of his fellow cardinal bishops, for instance, Damian was prepared to unleash his full learning on explicating the Biblical example of the prophet Gideon, but in the end, he decided to "explain the meaning of these complex stories more concisely, saying no more than is required for the type of discussion I began." (Ep. 69, 2:307).

In part, Damian had to keep things short precisely because he was writing letters, which required their authors to observe brevity as much as possible.[21] One way he accommodated that was by giving his readers shorter quotations and concise summaries instead of long block quotes or intricate theorizing, which is what you might find in a treatise or commentary. Near the conclusion of his first letter to Honestus, for instance, he remarked how he had refrained from "encumber[ing] you with complex and prolix arguments because I also know that you cannot carefully read through a great deal given your involvement in secular matters" (Ep. 1, 1:101–2). Interestingly, he took the same approach for clerics and monks who *did* have the time to read more extensively, even in matters that seemed to be most important for him. Take, for example, Ep. 112, his most comprehensive attempt to condemn the practice of clerical marriage. Then as now, readers would be forgiven for blanching at the almost overwhelming amount of theological, legal, and anecdotal evidence marshalled in this letter, but Damian steadfastly maintained that the letter gave only a small taste of what was possible. The Church Fathers were, he insisted, unanimous in their support of clerical celibacy. "But since no one will believe the words I say," he continued, "it is

21 Fletcher, "Rhetoric, Reform, and Christian Eloquence," 73–74.

necessary for me to put out a few of their words here, so that the little that comes off the top of my head might remind everyone how much more the Fathers say in agreement with this in their writings" (3:263).

Finally—and, I would argue, most importantly—Damian assured his students that they did not need to have the same amount of expertise as he did in order to understand what he was teaching them. This was especially the case with younger monks or laypeople, who lacked the experience or the time to master material in the way that seasoned hermits or monks could. Rather than ignoring these potential students, Damian adjusted his usually high standards for living the upright life to better suit their capabilities. A particularly clear example of this is Ep. 17, which was written to teach the nobleman T. (and, thus, any layperson) how to pray the monastic hours. Though he felt that it would be best for T. to pray exactly the same way that the monks did, he also knew they couldn't. So, while he provided a comprehensive explication of the canonical hours, he also offered T. some more realistic alternatives that would also make for a healthy prayer life. Instead of praying at all six canonical hours, for example, laypeople like T. could simply repeat the Lord's Prayer as they went about their day. Similarly, if they couldn't chant the entire Psalter every day (piece of cake, right?), they could make do with any Psalms they had access to, even if it was just one, repeated it as many times as needed (1:164).

In a nutshell, Damian's letters show us that he consciously chose to *not* write like the highly-trained intellectual that he was. Although the depth of his learning was obvious to anyone who knows how to look for it, he tried to restrain, or even hide it from audiences who might have found that intimidating. In other words, even though the letters are in an elite academic language, and even though they contain a lot of dense material that would be hard for a non-expert to get through, Damian did everything he could to make sure his audiences, whoever they were, found these letters accessible, understandable, and, most importantly of all, meaningful.

Embracing the Life of Service Conviction

What would it look like if medievalists today grounded their work in the Life of Service Conviction instead of the Life of the Mind Excuse? (I promise no one has to become a hermit and develop a near-debilitating fear of eternal damnation to do this.) Can you even imagine a public-facing, problem-solving, life-changing medieval studies? I don't think I could have done that in graduate school, but I learned to do it very quickly when I began my fellowship at the Newberry Library in 2016. Quite suddenly, I found myself responsible for spearheading an exhibition, developing digital resources, designing public programs, constructing a marketing campaign, and planning exhibition tours. I didn't know how to do *any* of those things, and my imposter syndrome really kicked on my first day, making me worry if being a medievalist had set me up for failure. But I had a job to do, so I just got started, and I quickly found that doing all these things I didn't know how to do was much easier than I expected. There were several factors for my success (especially my terrific and talented Newberry colleagues), but the most surprising one, the one it took me a while to notice, was my expertise in medieval culture.

Without any other formal training to guide me, I had to rely on what I already knew to get any of my work done, and what I knew best was how religious thinkers (including Peter Damian) wrote letters in the eleventh and twelfth centuries. So, when I needed to write exhibition labels describing the historical significance of a Newberry object in seventy-five words or less, I modelled it on how my letter-writers condensed complex theological explanations. Or, when I needed to imagine different types of digital resources, I thought about all the different genres you could find in any given eleventh- or twelfth-century letter collection. Also, when I was asked to present exhibition items to Newberry visitors in a collection presentation, I based my approach on the conversational signposting that I had seen time and time again in letters to laypeople or monastic novices. In other words, my medieval content expertise set me up for *success*, not failure. This experience was the first time that I had ever felt confident that what I knew as a medievalist was relevant outside the field. The same material that I was once embarrassed to talk about publicly was a huge reason why I was able to accomplish all sorts of things I had never done before, things that could make a difference at the Newberry and, importantly, for all the audiences it served.

That is what the Life of Service Conviction can do for you. The model Peter Damian left us in his letter collection can be, in my view, extremely helpful for you to figure out how to work it into every part of your medievalist career—how you understand your work, how you talk about it, and how you shape it. But at the beginning, I think the most important part of his model to highlight here is his belief that he could *do something* with the expert knowledge he had. Everything else that he did (or tried to do) as a professional intellectual rested on this single foundation, which set him up to impact his world in the way that he did. So, if you're having trouble imagining what medieval studies would look like under the Life of Service Conviction, just take a look at him. If you do, you won't see anything like Sad

Ovid; instead you'll see someone relentlessly charging out of his study and into the world to make whatever audiences he could find understand how his expert knowledge would change their lives.

I'm happy to say that there are already plenty of medievalists who are thinking of their expertise in the same way as Damian did. For example, more medievalists these days are willing to put their knowledge to work to unmask and discredit the dangerous myths about the Middle Ages weaponized by white supremacist groups.[22] Others are looking to identify and dismantle the harmful legacies of the field's nineteenth-century past that are still, as we've seen, holding us back from engaging the public as well as we could.[23] But for me, the group of medievalists that show the Life of Service Conviction the most these days are those working on the incredibly vital subfield of critical studies of race in the Middle Ages.[24] These are medievalists who consider themselves "an activist scholarly organization" whose work can show "the power of difference" in a field that sorely needs it.[25] Among professional medievalists, scholars of colour are much more willing to think about how their expert-level knowledge of the Middle Ages can help explain and even address the injustices and harms done by systemic racism today.[26]

Based on this, I'm convinced that a medieval studies that works according to the Life of Service Conviction is actually possible, which gives me hope that someday, I won't have to picture Sad Ovid whenever I think about the field. That's because, armed with this more active mindset, medievalists will, like Peter Damian, constantly be out in the world trying to make a difference. And the more we can do that, the more administrators, donors, students, and other stakeholders will realize that studying the Middle Ages is extremely relevant to the world today. And for me at least, the first signal that we're on the right track to that future won't be larger departments, more funding, or bigger grad student cohorts. All I'll need to see is a huddle of young graduate students at a conference wine hour, sharing stories about how they told some sceptical interrogators *exactly* what they were going to do with their PhD in medieval studies.

---

22 Lomuto, "Public Medievalism."

23 Cf. Gabriele and Perry, *The Bright Ages*, and Albin et al., eds., *Whose Middle Ages?*

24 For an overview, cf. Heng, *The Invention of Race in the European Middle Ages*; Whitaker, Otaño Gracia, and Fauvelle, eds., "Race, Race-Thinking, and Identity in the Global Middle Ages"; and Hsy and Orlemanski, *Race and Medieval Studies.*

25 Medievalists of Color, "Constitution," Article 1.2.

26 Cf. Whitaker, *Black Metaphors*, and Hsy, *Antiracist Medievalisms.*

Chapter 2

HILDEGARD OF BINGEN AND GENRE DIVERSITY

The Problem: Genre Dependency

One of my favourite things about going to a major medieval studies conference is the exhibition hall. I never get tired seeing a room filled with display after display of books in a variety of shapes, sizes, and colours, all of them promising to help me learn something new about the Middle Ages. From my first trip to the International Medieval Congress in Kalamazoo as an undergraduate, the "book room" always struck me as a terrific embodiment of my field and the work it was doing. But, the more that I think about it, I also have to admit that this very enjoyable spectacle of medieval scholarship is also a problem. After all, Sad Ovid is surrounded by a bunch of cool and interesting books, and they didn't seem to be doing him any good. I think that's because, from a public engagement perspective, all the books in those exhibition halls are basically the same.

Let me put it this way: the "book room" is the closest thing there is to visible, tangible evidence for "what medieval studies does." There is, of course, a lot more to the field that just those books, but the "book rooms" make it clear that these books are the most important manifestation of the field's work. So that means if you were going to, say, show that visible, tangible evidence to someone who wasn't a medievalist, this is what they would see: mostly shelves and tables of books that, no matter their subject, invariably include complex, well-structured arguments; detailed overviews of scholarly conversations; a steady dose of academic jargon specific to a given field; and extensive notes featuring liberal amounts of original languages. In other words, these non-medievalists would see a bunch of scholarly publications. While I enjoy scholarly publications (and all their constituent parts) very much, they are not terribly exciting to anyone who isn't a professional medievalist or on their way to becoming one. So, if a room full of scholarly publications is the best way for us to show off what medieval studies does to people outside the field, it's no wonder we're in such trouble.

I've now come to see that the book-filled exhibition halls I love so much are, in fact, a symptom of a structural roadblock holding medievalists back from doing better public engagement: Genre Dependency, a term I use to describe our field's widespread prioritization and valorization of a single genre for sharing our collective knowledge and expertise with other audiences. Compared to the other structural roadblocks we talk about in this book, I think this might be the sneakiest one. In fact, I'd wager that most medievalists at any level don't realize it's a problem at all. I certainly didn't when I was in graduate school; at no point in my training did I ever think about sharing what I knew about medieval letter-writing in anything other than a monograph or journal article. Everything about the academic system—the advice I got from professors, the requirements for my degree (i.e., a dissertation), job talks, expectations for tenure portfolios, and, not least, what I saw in those exhibition halls when I went to conferences—made it perfectly clear that writing well-structured, thoroughly-researched, properly articulated studies that were approved by other expert scholars was the most important thing professional medievalists did. Full stop. Scholarly publications are, of course, terrific tools for taking deep dives into medieval culture that can reveal tons of useful information, and I want to avoid a future for the field in which they don't exist. But for that to happen, I'm convinced that we need to change the current situation, in which the field considers them the most important thing that exists.

In this chapter, I'll explain how this over-valorization of the scholarly publication is setting the field up for public engagement failure by limiting the ways in which audiences who aren't scholars can access the field. Against this, I'll discuss how medieval intellectuals took the opposite approach; namely, by giving equal value to any and all creative means by which they could express their expertise. Then, I'll discuss how I've seen the medieval approach in full force through the fortunes of the Newberry bookstore during an exhibition on the medieval and early modern roots of race.

When you really think about it, there's no reason why Genre Dependency should be a problem for medieval studies. There are countless possibilities for how medievalists *could* express their knowledge about the medieval past. Literally any means humans have developed to communicate is at our disposal, and there is no reason why any of those other options are better than any others. Yet in practice, it's clear that when we as a field imagine what medievalists do (or, perhaps better, *should* do), the esoteric scholarly monograph reigns supreme. That, after all, is precisely the genre of the dissertation, which every graduate student is expected to produce at the end of their training. After that, anyone fortunate enough to actually secure a job in academia, especially at R1 universities, knows perfectly well that their advancement to tenure depends largely, if not exclusively, on peer-reviewed, scholarly publications. And for those who *don't* secure those jobs, the expectation to try and write monographs and articles remains. Again, it doesn't have to be this way. Professors could decide that genres other than the standard dissertation could demonstrate how well graduate students have mastered the required skills of the field, departments could decide that more creative and accessible formats could count for tenure, and independent scholars or medievalists at teaching colleges could be confident that their non-scholarly-publication work also counts as doing the work of a medievalist. But for the most part, none of these things happens nearly often enough. And for that, we have Genre Dependency to blame.

In part because it's so sneaky, this roadblock does more damage than many of us realize. First, it prevents us from building productive connections with non-academic audiences, because scholarly publications aren't terribly exciting, interesting, or valuable for people outside of academia, who don't typically have the time or skills necessary to get the most out of them. Second (and perhaps more dangerously), Genre Dependency creates the illusion that there is only one way to *truly* be a practicing medievalist: namely, to acquire a professional position that allows you to write scholarly publications, which is almost exclusively limited to the academic system itself (including museums and research libraries). That, in turn, makes the legions of PhDs who don't get those positions feel like they're no longer full participants in their field, because how could you call yourself a medievalist if you can't research and write monographs and journal articles?[1] Finally, and most damaging of all, Genre Dependency makes the idea of becoming a professional medievalist less appealing for many people; if you love the Middle Ages but hate the idea of writing a monograph, you're going to find something else to do with your life.

In other words, Genre Dependency is another factor that makes medieval studies seem irrelevant to so many potential stakeholders outside academia (and even quite a few within it); if the most visible and valorized expression of what medieval studies does strikes you as boring or inaccessible, then why bother supporting it at all? So, as much as I will always love going into an exhibition hall packed to the gills with medieval scholarship, if the field is to survive, we need to find a way to make sure that *other* visible expressions of medieval expertise are represented equally in that same room. That is, the field needs to make it clear that genres that audiences outside academia find accessible and desirable are celebrated and valued just as much as scholarly publications. We need, in other words, to leave Genre

1 Caccipuoti and Keohane-Burbridge, "Introduction," 17.

Dependency behind, and embrace the possibilities that come with expressing our expertise using formats that people find compelling, interesting, and...dare I say it...fun. That can be a scary thing, to be sure, considering how long we've depended on the scholarly publication to define what we do. But I'm here to tell you that avoiding Genre Dependency is not at all new; in fact, it's downright medieval.

The Medieval Solution: Genre Diversity

This might seem an odd claim at first. After all, when we look at the visible manifestations of intellectual culture in medieval Europe, we find a lot of books, many of which are just as ordered, thoroughly-researched, and densely packed with sources and analysis as any scholastic publication today. Still, I believe that professional medieval intellectuals would have found present-day medievalists' Genre Dependency problem to be a bit odd, if not confusing. While a lot of them wrote a lot of long treatises, that genre didn't have the same dominance in their culture that the scholarly publication has in ours.

If we take a more comprehensive view of medieval intellectuals' work, it's clear that they had much less of an issue using their imagination when it came to sharing their expertise. Though much of their production comes down to us in the form of written texts, those texts were only one part of a rich culture of learning, reading, and instruction that also drew heavily on oral culture, the performing arts, visual art and architecture, music, nature, the memory arts, and plenty of other non-textual things.[2] Your standard intellectual in medieval Europe saw all these things as raw material that could be used to invent various pathways to higher understanding or experience of the divine, and there was no assumption that one genre of written text was the best route for all those pathways to travel through.[3] On the contrary, when intellectuals were ready to share the results of that intense, imaginative work, everything was fair game: scholastic treatises of course, but also romances and other imaginative fiction, studies of nature, architecture, visual art, poetry, dramatic performances, and so much more.[4] As opposed to Genre Dependency, then, medieval European intellectual culture was defined by Genre Diversity.

---

2 Ohly, *Sensus spiritualis*.

3 Carruthers, *The Craft of Thought*.

4 Carruthers, ed., *Rhetoric Beyond Words*.

While many intellectuals probably felt most comfortable expressing their knowledge in just one genre or format, given what we know about the intellectual culture in which they participated, it's highly unlikely any of them would have thought, much less insisted, that there was one best genre for them to use when sharing their expertise. If we want to get past the roadblock of Genre Dependency, then, we need to start doing the same. And we should do that because, as we'll see more clearly in our model for this chapter, sharing one's knowledge in multiple genres and formats also creates multiple points of access for different audiences to not only receive that expertise, but also to *understand* it.

In what follows, we'll take a closer look at the practice of medieval Genre Diversity. We'll try to understand why medieval intellectuals felt it was important to express their knowledge in different ways, and, more importantly, how they attempted to do so. As we'll see, this was not a cut-and-dry process; authors and creators had to think carefully about what genres to use, and then work diligently to shape their content based on the requirements of whatever they chose. By seeing that in action, we can get a better sense of how medievalists today can start thinking about diversifying the ways in which we share our own expertise. Thankfully, we won't have to launch into an exhaustive overview of medieval European intellectual culture to do all of that. As it happens, all we have to do is turn to one especially remarkable medieval intellectual who, maybe more than anyone else, was determined to share her expertise in every possible way she could.

The Model: Hildegard of Bingen

If you ask me, Hildegard of Bingen (1098–1179) is the most extraordinary person from the entire European Middle Ages. Born to a free noble family in the German Rhineland, she entered the monastic life as a young girl, joining an enclosed community of nuns at the Benedictine monastery of St. Disibod in the upper Rhine, and eventually took over as *magistra* for this community when she was thirty-eight. Then, starting in about 1152 (when she was in her early fifties) everything changed. Hildegard became an instant celebrity, and began doing all kinds of things that were supposed to be impossible for women in her day: she wrote works under her own name, preached in public, defied and criticized high-ranking ecclesiastical and secular leaders, and founded not one, but *two* new convents after getting her enclosed community out of St. Disibod, serving as the de facto abbess of the convent of Rupertsberg near the town of Bingen am Rhein.[5] When she died in 1179, she was widely venerated as a saint throughout the German lands, and was finally elevated to sainthood and declared a doctor of the church in 2012.

How did she do all of this? Well, if you asked her, Hildegard would probably have told you that she didn't really have a choice. In fact, she probably would have told you that she, strictly speaking, didn't actually do any of it at all. In her telling, her incredible public career actually began around 1141, when, as she reported in her first visionary treatise, she saw "the incredible splendor of a heavenly vision" and heard "a voice from Heaven" commanding her to "speak these things that you see and hear, but do not write them in the way you, or any other person, want, but according to the will of the one who understands, sees, and ordains all things in the secrets of His mysteries" (*Scivias*, 3).[6] From that moment on (though it took her awhile to go public with it), she was no longer a simple *magistra* of a small community of nuns in the Rhineland, but a transmitter of commands, messages, and instruction that came directly from God, in the form of what she described as "the Living Light" (*lux uiuens*). Hildegard was no ordinary medieval intellectual: she was a *prophet.* As many scholars have noted, this status was the key to her "staggering" accomplishments: it was the source of the drive and determination she required to achieve her goals, the protection she needed to do work that only highly-trained male clerics were supposed to be able to do, and an effective way to attract the attention of audiences far beyond (and, hierarchically speaking, far *above*) her local community.[7]

At first glance, this prophetic status might seem to disqualify Hildegard as a professional intellectual for contemporary medievalists to emulate. Indeed, she herself may well have completely rejected that idea. In her works, she consistently made a clear distinction between herself and the educated clerics, monks, and prelates of her day. Unlike them, she was "unlearned" (*indocta*); in fact, she insisted that the Living Light chose her specifically because she was "not well-versed in the Scriptures, nor instructed by any teacher on this earth" (*Scivias* 3.11.18:586). Scholars today agree with her

5 Overviews include Newman, ed., *Voice of the Living Light*; Kienzle et al., eds., *A Companion to Hildegard of Bingen*; and Bain, ed., *The Cambridge Companion to Hildegard of Bingen*.

6 I'll be using the *Scivias* a lot in this chapter. Citations from it come from Adelgundis Führkötter's critical edition, and will include the book, vision number, chapter and page number from the edition (e.g., *Scivias*, 3.11.18:586).

7 Cf. Newman, "Visions and Validations," and Dronke, "Hildegard of Bingen," 144–201.

to a point—she likely did not have the same intensive course of study as her male contemporaries and her own Latin skills were a bit rough—but overall, it's clear that she was every bit the professional intellectual the learned (and exclusively male) clerics of her day were.[8] Her duties as the *magistra* meant that she was expected to be able to read and write in Latin and know Scripture well enough to be able to explain it to her spiritual charges.[9] More than that, though she didn't openly cite them, her work shows she must have known a good deal of theology as well, from the classic Church Fathers up to cutting-edge contemporary religious thinkers like Bernard of Clairvaux and Hugh of Saint-Victor.[10]

Most importantly for us, though, Hildegard's prophetic persona has a lot to teach us about cultivating Genre Diversity. In some ways, you could say that her entire public career depended on it. For all its unquestionably practical advantages, Hildegard primarily understood her prophetic status as a calling that *required* her to intervene in the world around her (hi there, Life of Service Conviction!), a world in which everyone (clergy, monks, nobility, peasants) had become increasingly lazy, distracted, and ignorant of the commands of divine justice.[11] Her mission, according to the Living Light, was to make a real difference in all of their lives: "Therefore burst out like an abundant spring and flow out with so much mystical knowledge," it commanded her, "that those who consider you contemptible because of Eve's sin *will be stirred up* thanks to this flood's irrigation" (*Scivias* 1.1.0:8, my emphasis). This commitment to action and reform set Hildegard apart from other medieval visionaries before and after her.[12] We can get a sense of that in a woodcut from a compilation of medieval visionaries printed in 1513, which includes Hildegard's first visionary treatise.[13] Unlike the other visionaries (three men and two women), who simply behold their heavenly visions mostly empty-handed, Hildegard carries a book (representing her many writings) and a small model of an abbey church (representing the two convents she founded). This portrait

8 Dronke, "Hildegard of Bingen," 148–49.

9 Kienzle, *Hildegard of Bingen and her Gospel Homilies*, 30–35.

10 Ginther, "Hildegard of Bingen's Theology," 93.

11 Cf. Newman, "Introduction," 12, and Dronke, "Hildegard of Bingen," 146.

12 Cf. Newman, "Visions and Validations," 172–75; Van Engen, "Letters and the Public Persona of Hildegard," and Anderson, "The Context and Reception of Hildegard of Bingen's Visions," 190–95.

13 Hildegard of Bingen et al, *Liber trium virorum et trium spiritualium virginum*, Wolfenbüttel, Herzog August Bibliothek, A: 456.11 Theol. 2° (1).

reminds us that, even more than three centuries after her death, people still knew her as a visionary who *got stuff done* (Fig. 2).

Of course, as with any intellectual in her day, her writings were key to her success, and it's that body of work that now stands, in my humble opinion, as the best witness we have for the practice of medieval Genre Diversity. In them, Hildegard left one of the most diverse bodies of surviving work of any intellectual from the European Middle Ages. It includes a trilogy of long theological treatises, an unusually large collection of letters, a series of exegetical sermons, works of medicine and natural science, music, drama, and even a mysterious new language. The variety is astonishing all by itself, and Hildegard and her team took steps to ensure that future generations would recognize that.[14]

Towards the end of her life, she and a team of scribes, editors, and secretaries began work on an official, physical record of her dedication to Genre Diversity in the form of a manuscript codex containing of most of Hildegard's written work, now known as the *Riesencodex* (Wiesbaden, Hochschul- und Landesbibliothek RheinMain: Hs. 2). Planned with Hildegard's full participation and completed after her death, this volume was supposed to aid the inevitable effort to canonize her by providing a definitive record of the all the work she had done in the service of the Living Light. Though it doesn't include all of her works (her writings on natural science and medicine are noticeably absent), the manuscript makes clear that Genre Diversity was an essential part of that faithful service. In order, the *Riesencodex* includes a trilogy of visionary treatises (*Scivias, Liber vitae meritorum, Liber divinorum operum*), a letter to the prelates in Mainz demanding that they lift an interdict on her community (*Epistola ad praelatos Moguntinos*), a biography (*Vitae Hildegardis*), a large letter collection (*Epistolarium*), a series of exegetical sermons on the Gospels (*Expositio Evangeliorum*), a dictionary of the language she invented (*Lingua ignota*), a series of liturgical chants (*Symphoniae*), and a dramatic performance set to music (*Ordo virtutum*).[15]

In other words, the diversity of the *Riesencodex*'s contents proves that Hildegard took her calling so seriously that she shared her prophetic message in practically every written or artistic genre she possibly could, something that was meant to be a sure sign of her sanctity. But for us, the contents

---

14 Schrader and Führkötter, *Die Echtheit des Schrifttums.*

15 https://hlbrm.digitale-sammlungen.hebis.de/handschriften-hlbrm/content/titleinfo/449618.

Figure 2. Hildegard displays the proof of her productivity on the title page woodcut for the *Liber trium virorum et trium spiritualium virginum*. Wolfenbüttel, Herzog August Bibliothek, A: 456.11 Theol. 2° (1). Photograph by author. Courtesy of the Herzog August Bibliothek.

of the *Riesencodex* are also something else: a meticulously-curated record of her commitment to Genre Diversity. In it, we can understand the nuts and bolts of what Hildegard had to do to successfully get her message across in different formats, and how she understood the value of each one of those. After all, though medieval authors had a less-stringent sense of genre than we do today, they still understood that different formats had their own rhetorical characteristics and forms that determined how accessible they were to various audiences.[16] Every text in the *Riesencodex* expressed Hildegard's prophetic message, but not always in exactly the same way. As we'll see, it's in those subtle yet unmistakable differences that we'll be able to make out a path leading away from Genre Dependency.

Approaching Hildegard's Genre Diversity

We'll need to start with Hildegard's prophetic message, because it was this that compelled her to practice so much Genre Diversity. Like virtually every other professional intellectual of her day, Hildegard's mission was ultimately about helping people get to heaven through understanding divine truths, though in concert with the more conservative strand of spiritual reform that was sweeping through the twelfth-century Latin Church. In particular, she was interested in upholding the spiritual structures that led humans to salvation by convincing people to adopt the beliefs and practices that embodied them in the world.[17] For her, those were firmly rooted in the values of traditional Benedictine monasticism, and her prophetic mission was, in large part, dedicated to making sure those values were fully understood, appreciated, and practiced by clergy and laity alike. This, in a nutshell, is what she does in all her visionary work, including everything in the *Riesencodex*.

Now, although her message was very clearly orthodox and traditional (which is why she was able talk about it publicly at all), Hildegard shared it in a way that was entirely her own, namely, by reading salvation history through the lenses of femininity and the materiality of Creation and explaining it with her unique poetic and literary abilities.[18] Since we don't have time to go through every detail of Hildegard's mission here, we'll focus on just one monastic virtue that she felt her world very much needed: humility. This was one of the most fundamental cultural values in Christian religious life, includ-

---

16 See the various publications in the Typologie des sources du Moyen Âge occidental series from Brepols.

17 Fletcher, "'Understand, Delight, and Obey,'" 242–98.

18 Cf. Newman, *Sister of Wisdom,* and Ginther, "Hildegard of Bingen's Theology."

ing (spoiler alert!) in the Benedictine order.[19] Hildegard herself referred to humility as "the Queen of the Virtues" (*regina Virtutum*) multiple times throughout her writings, and many scholars have noted that the virtue was the bedrock of her entire prophetic persona.[20] Not surprisingly, promoting the widespread cultivation of humility was an essential part of Hildegard's reform program, and it shows up consistently in all of her visionary work.

So how does humility show up in the texts of the *Riesencodex*? Again for the sake of time, we'll focus on three that will give us a solid sense of how Hildegard shaped her expression of this cornerstone virtue in different ways. We'll begin with Hildegard's first visionary treatise, the *Scivias* (a contraction of *Scite vias domini*, or "know the ways of the Lord"). The *Scivias* consists of twenty-six visions arranged into three books of unequal length, which respectively deal with the Creator and Creation (six visions), the Redeemer (seven visions), and salvation history visualized as the construction of a building by the virtues (thirteen visions). This was the work that introduced Hildegard to the world, and was arguably her most important, so naturally it comes first in the *Riesencodex*. Next, we'll look at the *Epistolarium*, a massive collection of over 390 letters written by Hildegard or addressed to her, one of the largest to survive from the twelfth century.[21] The *Epistolarium* shows Hildegard as a prophet in action—instructing, consoling, and criticizing individuals from all throughout the social and ecclesiastical hierarchies, usually through visions or in the voice of the Living Light.[22] Finally, we'll look at the *Ordo virtutum* (The Order of Virtues), a musical drama that Hildegard composed at about the same time she was finishing the *Scivias* in the early 1150s.[23] This piece, the only surviving medieval musical drama whose author/composer we know, tells the story of the Soul (*Anima*), who falls away from the spiritual life through the Devil's seductions, but comes back again through the assistance of the personified Virtues. Taken together, these three distinct expressions of what Hildegard knew—treatise, letter, and sung drama—helped multiple audiences see and

19 *RB 1980*, 32–38.

20 Cf. Dronke, "Hildegard of Bingen," 90–91 and Newman, "Sybil," 19.

21 Evidence from the *Epistolarium* is from Lievan van Acker and Monika Klaes's three-volume edition of the *Epistolarium*; the citations will include the letter number, volume of the edition, and page number (e.g., Ep. 18r, 1:54).

22 Cf. Ferrante, "Correspondent," and Fletcher, "Reading Hildegard of Bingen's Letters."

23 Citations from this text are pretty straightforward; they simply reference the page number in Peter Dronke's critical edition.

understand the concept of humility in three unique ways.[24] To put it briefly, the *Scivias* gives us a deep expression of humility that is supposed to be *contemplated*, the *Epistolae* gives us a direct expression that is supposed to be *heard* and *obeyed*, and the *Ordo* gives us an embodied expression that needs to be *felt*.

Seeing Humility in Hildegard's Work

Let's start with the *Scivias*, which presents humility through the esoteric, highly structured, and dense genre of the theological treatise. Humility is found all over this work, but nowhere more clearly than in the eighth vision of the third book. This vision describes a great pillar Hildegard saw on the south side of the great building of salvation, which represented the humanity of the incarnate Son of God. Going up and down the pillar were "all the virtues of God" happily carrying stones to build the building. Seven virtues, standing for the seven gifts of the Holy Spirit, stood out from that multitude, and of these, Humility was "the first one." Accordingly, she has the most elaborately-detailed appearance: unlike the other Virtues described in the vision, Humility "wore a woman's veil on her head and a robe of transparent crystal" and "a golden crown with three high prongs that was covered with most precious green and red gems and many shining white pearls. On her chest she also had an incredibly bright mirror, in which the image of the incarnate Son of God appeared with wonderful clarity" (3.8.0:478–79). In addition to this, Humility is also the first Virtue to speak to Hildegard, describing herself as "the pillar of humble minds and the destroyer of prideful hearts" (3.8.1:479).

The concept of humility comes across rather differently in the *Epistolarium*, which, as we've already seen with Peter Damian, had a completely different rhetorical focus. Instead of dense arguments and piles of citations, letters demanded a more concise, focused, and personalized approach to sharing information. And yet, Hildegard and her editors wanted to make it clear that her letters were even *more* personal than others. They do so by including a substantial number of Hildegard's direct responses to incoming letters (the edition even marks these letters with a small "r"), thereby giving the reader a clearer sense of how she interacted with her audiences.[25] Accordingly, since each of the letters in Hildegard's collection was written for a particular individual or group, there is not the same degree of unity

24 Zátonyi, *Vidi et intellexi.*

25 Van Acker, "Der Briefwechsel der heiligen Hildegard."

in terms of format or content across the letters as there is in the *Scivias*. That said, it's clear we're still talking about the same virtue here: humility in the letters remains the "first flower" of the spiritual life, and practicing it in the world helps to build "the living tabernacle in the heavenly Jerusalem" (Ep. 262, 3:11). What's different is *how* we see humility expressed. True to the action-oriented epistolary genre, instead of a personification like in the *Scivias*, the "queen of virtues" appears much more often in the *Epistolarium* as a *modifier*, that is, the way in which Hildegard's recipients were supposed to do whatever the Living Light commanded. A lot of the time, humility works as an adverb, like when Hildegard explained to Abbot Adam of Ebrach that "Whoever relies on humbly (*humilitate*) practicing the virtues… will have the grace of God" (Ep. 85r/b, 1:208). At other times, we find humility as an adjective used to describe the other virtues critical to Hildegard's reform program, like when a prior learned that the sacraments needed to be administered "with humble obedience" (*cum humili obedientia*) (Ep. 84r, 1:195–96). Regardless of what part of speech it was, we tend to see humility in short, direct commands and/or instructions, usually following imperative commands (e.g., *audite, intelligite, cauete, resiste, disce*). Humility also comes out in the *Epistolarium* through its absence; in many letters, Hildegard advocates for more humility by stressing that its opposite vice, pride (*superbia*), is the cause of whatever problems Hildegard's correspondents are experiencing. A particularly good example comes from a letter to Archbishop Henry of Mainz, in which the "Spirit of God" told the archbishop (and other prelates besides) that "your cursed, malicious, and threatening words are not heard by anyone, for in this way your staffs, raised up in haughty pride, do not stretch out towards God, but to the disgraceful punishments of your presumptuous desires" (Ep. 18r, 1:54).

We find a bit of a different situation in the *Ordo virtutum*, which, unlike the other two works, was meant to be a physical, multimedia performance. Here again we see humility as a personified figure, and one of the main characters in the drama, to boot. Considering how they were completed at the same time, it's no surprise that the presentation of Humility in the *Ordo* has some strong resonances with the *Scivias*.[26] Unlike the treatise, though, Humility is much more visible here, which is something we should expect in genre that was originally supposed to be literally staged. Though she isn't always the focus of the action, at no point in the performance would the audiences *not* see Humility on stage doing something. Even when she is not

26 Fassler, "Allegorical Architecture."

the centre of attention, like at the beginning and end of the play, audiences would have seen her standing and singing with the other Virtues. But overall, there's no question that Humility is the leader of the group. When the Devil taunts the virtues after the Soul leaves the stage to enjoy the world, she is the one who responds: "I and my soldiers know exactly who you are: that ancient dragon who wished to fly above the Most High, but God himself cast you into the abyss" (509). From there Humility takes centre stage for most of the rest of the action, identifying herself as "I, Humility, Queen of the Virtues" (*Ego, Humilitas, regina Virtutum*), and calling on the other Virtues to join the effort to resist the Devil and bring the Soul back home (509). And, when the dishevelled and suffering Soul returns to the stage, seeking forgiveness and repentance, guess who she calls on first? "And o true medicine Humility, come to my aid...Now I run to you, so that you may take me up" (517). Finally, it's Humility who calls the Soul to her and commands the Virtues to bind the Devil, even throwing in some good encouragement along the way ("Bind that Devil, o illustrious Virtues!") (519).

Understanding Humility in Hildegard's Works

From this quick overview, it's clear that we're dealing with three distinct expressions of the same virtue, each of which creates a different pathway for the viewer/reader/listener to *understand* humility and its significance. Let's go back to the treatise first. Seeing Humility is very easy in the *Scivias*, but understanding it is another matter. Like any divine vision received by a prophet, this presentation of humility is not supposed to be clear-cut; the visual and textual symbolism can be very confusing at first glance, something that Hildegard's medieval readers noticed (e.g., Ep. 244, 2:524). Readers would have to do a particular kind of work to understand what Humility is doing in this vision: exegesis, the slow, meticulous parsing of a source in order to reveal the meanings hidden beneath the surface of a text or object. To put it another way, expressing humility through a treatise means that the reader will have to do *a lot* of work to understand it. Every vision in the *Scivias* is set up in a way that encourages this kind of engagement: first we get a careful, detailed description of what Hildegard saw, and then a thorough and methodical explanation of the spiritual meaning of each element of the vision, all the while bringing in references to Scripture, hagiography, parables, and other sources as necessary. Humility actually starts this exegetical process herself in *Scivias* 3.8, proclaiming right away that "Whoever wishes to imitate me, desiring to be my child and yearning to embrace me as a mother, by completing my work with my help, they will step onto the foundation and peacefully make their way up to the highest things" (479). Reading on a bit, we learn that Humility's instructions mirror the significance of Christ's humanity (represented by the pillar), which laid out precisely how individuals could make their way to a holy life (495). More details come when the Living Light explains the meaning of Humility's appearance. The veil and crystal-like mantle she wears symbolizes how she "humbly wears the chain of subjection to God, and with heavenly concern strikes down the haughty devil" (3.8.17:503). She wears a gold crown because she "first manifested the Savior" in the Incarnation, and its other features respectively symbolize important points of Christological doctrine, namely the Trinity (the three prongs), Christ's ministry (the green gems), Christ's passion (the red gems), and the resurrection and ascension (white pearls). And finally, the mirror she wears is a reminder of how God is reflected in all Humility's works, thereby making her the "most solid foundation of all good works that men do" (3.8.18:505–6).

Understanding humility takes a lot less work in the *Epistolarium*, which is exactly what medieval letters were supposed to do. Like Damian's "nails and goads," letters were designed to make people *do* things, and that's what we find in her letter collection. As we've seen, the virtue doesn't appear as a personified virtue, so much less exegesis is required to understand it when Hildegard invokes it. Instead, the format here is what I would call *personalized* instruction about why humility matters. To give us a better idea of how this works, let's focus on a particular situation that people repeatedly brought to Hildegard's attention: what to do when the leader of your spiritual community is being too harsh.[27] This, of course, had been a problem since the early days of Christian monasticism, but it was becoming more prevalent in the twelfth century, when the foundation of new monastic orders offered monks and nuns more options for their spiritual life. So, if one form of monastic life wasn't working for you (say, because your abbot was too strict), you could just choose another one. Hildegard, however, wasn't having it. In her responses to these queries, she was adamant that God had intentionally placed everyone into a specific spot in the spiritual hierarchy, and no one was allowed to disrupt the divine plan by doing something else.[28] According to the letters, humility was key to maintaining that order. For example, the Living Light reminded a monk named Berthold that

---

27 Ferrante, "Correspondent," 94–99, and Fletcher, "Reading Hildegard's Letters," 118–19.

28 Fletcher, "'Understand, Delight, and Obey,'" 289–96.

he was required to "humbly obey [his abbot] as much as you are able," even if his demands seemed harsh (Ep. 218, 2:478). At other times, Hildegard tried to show how using humility could help improve the situation in a strict monastery, such as in the script she offered to a congregation of monks suffering under a harsh abbot: "humble yourself before him in humble devotion, saying, 'Father, Father, we cannot bear this, and we pray you will spare us from this...'" (Ep. 59, 1:141). That said, Hildegard was not about to just let abbots and abbesses do whatever they wanted; they also had to "ensure that all of your works are done in true humility" to make life easier for their spiritual charges (Ep. 118, 2:291). In all these cases, guided by the rhetorical requirements of the letter form, Hildegard attempted to convince her recipients that they could make their spiritual troubles go away if they started being humble *right away*.

We find the easiest (relatively speaking) path to understanding humility in the *Ordo virtutum*, even though we're again dealing with a female personification whose appearance and personality were heavily informed by, if not outright copied from, the *Scivias*.[29] But even with those similarities, the *Ordo*'s viewers experienced humility in an entirely different way. I say that because, unlike in the treatise or any of the letters, the *Ordo*'s viewers see Humility in the flesh, standing before them as a living, breathing, moving, and singing person. The drama format allowed Hildegard to "embody" the virtue in the drama, thereby making its invisible spiritual function (as the foundation of all other virtuous activity) visible for the audience, which more than makes up for the general lack of detail about Humility and her qualities in the actual text of the work.[30] Instead of contemplating dense descriptions of how humility was the divine antidote to the pride that caused the fall of Lucifer and Mankind, the *Ordo*'s viewers saw Humility snapping back at the Devil's taunts and enthusiastically commanding Victory to "run with your troops and together bind this devil!" (517). Similarly, instead of receiving short direct reminders that humility was the key to a successful spiritual life, the viewers would see the Queen of Virtues compassionately welcoming back, and possibly even physically embracing, the forlorn Soul after its disastrous time in the world: "O miserable daughter, I, the great healer, wish to embrace you, because you have suffered harsh and bitter wounds" (517). In short, the *Ordo virtutum* is primarily interested in bringing the virtue of humility to life, in order to make an instantly legible model that viewers

29 Cf. Fassler, "Allegorical Architecture" and Meconi, *Hildegard of Bingen*, 19–26.

30 Altstatt, "The *Ordo virtutum* and Benedictine Monasticism."

could imitate, in precisely the way that monastic superiors were supposed to be living models for their subordinates.[31]

Creating More Access through Genre Diversity

So, after this very short overview, what can we say about Hildegard's Genre Diversity? Broadly speaking, I think it's clear that this particular approach was essential for helping a variety of audiences hear and be transformed by her prophetic message. The *Scivias* is the most obviously prophetic presentation; here we see a meticulously detailed but enigmatic personification that resists simple understanding, and thus must be explained bit by bit. In the letters, on the contrary, humility shows up mostly as a modifier (adverb or adjective) in concise, direct commands and explanations that advocate for certain types of human actions. Then, in the *Ordo virtutum*, we literally see Humility in an embodied performance that interacts with other characters and physically does a lot more things (singing, rebuking, consoling, and commanding).

None of this was by accident, of course. The different expressions of humility we see here were rooted in the particular rhetorical characteristics of each genre Hildegard used. The *Scivias*, unique as it was, clearly drew on two staple genres of Christian theology: the commentary and the *summa*. We can see the former in the format of the visions in *Scivias*, which set forth a base text (in this case, her vision instead of a Biblical passage) followed by a comprehensive, well-sourced explanation of that text's hidden meaning(s).[32] We see the latter, the cutting edge of theology in the twelfth century, in the *Scivias*'s ambition to systematically explain the nature of everything in the world and salvation history through a highly-ordered, progressive presentation of material.[33] In Hildegard's day, commentaries and *summae* were the best genres for supporting deep dives into any theological or religious topic, and they both demanded considerable time, effort, and outside knowledge to fully understand.

That level of engagement, however, did not fly with medieval letters. Twelfth-century intellectuals understood perfectly well that letters, even the ones that deal with theological matters, had to make their point as concisely as possible, so that they would have the best chance of convincing

31 Von Moos, *Geschichte als Topik*.

32 Newman, "Visions and Validations," 24.

33 Cf. Newman, "Introduction," 23, and Ginther, "Hildegard of Bingen's Theology," 88.

their addressee to think or do something. They were okay with sacrificing that level of detail, though, because doing so allowed them to create a direct, almost tangible connection with an individual recipient, which could significantly heighten a letter's persuasive ability.[34] Based on the incoming correspondence in Hildegard's collection, this fundamental aspect of the medieval epistolary genre made Hildegard's letters especially desirable, because they could create a personal connection to the Living Light itself.[35] The goal here was not to give these audiences something that they would need to diligently contemplate (though they could do that, too), but something that would quickly and decisively convince them to base all their thoughts and actions on humility.

The *Ordo virtutum* represented something else entirely: a full-fledged multimedia experience incorporating the visual (costumed actors moving around) and the aural (music and spoken words).[36] This was precisely the sort of thing that occurred in all Latin Christian worship services, which combined a variety of forms of artistic expression in order to bring people into the different religious ceremonies.[37] By Hildegard's time, a number of performances that represented certain parts of the liturgy had been developed to highlight the historical and theological connections to particularly important moments in salvation history, and the *Ordo* fit snugly into this larger tradition.[38] This is also why the music mattered; as many scholars have noted, Hildegard used musical performances as a way to emphasize different "invisible" things in more approachable ways, such as when Victory announces the successful binding of the devil with what Margot Fassler calls "an unusually high *Gaudete*."[39] In that sense, the *Ordo* used art as a way to *move* its viewers to imitate Humility through their emotional responses, more so than their intellectual ones.

So why did Hildegard bother with all this? Why not just talk about humility in her visionary treatises and be done with it? Hildegard understood that each of these expressions of humility, shaped as they were by the rhetorical nature of their genre, would be particularly (though not exclusively) useful for specific audiences. I think it's safe to say that the *Scivias*

34 Fletcher, "Rhetoric, Reform, and Christian Eloquence," 73–74.

35 Van Engen, "Letters and the Public Persona," 416–17.

36 Enders, "Visions with Voices."

37 Heffernan and Matter, eds., *The Liturgy of the Medieval Church*.

38 Rankin, "Liturgical Drama."

39 Fassler, "Allegorical Architecture," 221–22.

was designed to speak to experts, that is, professional intellectuals who had the time and the skills to work through complex, lengthy, systematic presentations of material that treatises and commentaries offered. In fact, we learn in the first vision of the *Scivias* that it was precisely *this* group that was failing to do their jobs properly, so Hildegard packaged the command for them to shape up in a format that was quite familiar to them (1.1.0:8). Letters, on the contrary, could be adapted to fit the needs of any kind of audience, and Hildegard took full advantage of that fact to tailor her prophetic message specifically for individuals who asked for them (along with some who didn't). It also allowed her to make sure that the mysteries unveiled in the treatises like *Scivias* actually reached the individuals who most needed to hear them, but in the shorter, more personalized, and more convincing presentation that the letter form offered.[40] For its part, the *Ordo* probably had the smallest, most circumscribed intentional audience of them all: Hildegard's community of nuns at the Rupertsberg. The number of parts in the play correspond exactly to the number of nuns Hildegard had with her at the convent in 1152, and the considerable differences in the length and complexity of the characters' parts suggests strongly that they were written for specific singers.[41] The *Ordo* gave these viewers an introduction to humility that was especially tailored to their needs; indeed, the Soul's complaints about the difficulty of the spiritual life probably sounded a lot like what young and inexperienced nuns might have said early in their spiritual career. The expression of a key monastic virtue like humility through a sung drama would have been an effective way to get the importance of this virtue across to people like these young nuns, who didn't yet have the training to work their way through a longer, denser presentation like in the *Scivias*.

In a nutshell, Hildegard's multi-faceted approach to teaching others about humility explains why Genre Diversity was so important to her mission. The best way to ensure that everyone heard and understood her prophetic message of reform was to share that message in as many ways as possible. On practical level, that would help her "stir up" a variety of audiences by giving them formats that suited their interests and capabilities, but it would also allow her to express the divine truths she saw more fully and comprehensively. After all, the three expressions of humility here are not *exclusive*, but *complementary*; anyone who read all these works would have a much more complete understanding of the spiritual importance of humil-

40 Fletcher, "Reading Hildegard's Letters," 112.

41 Meconi, *Hildegard of Bingen*, 23.

ity than if they had read only one. But she also must have known that only a very few readers would have been able to read everything she wrote, so she made sure that each individual work was able to fulfil her prophetic mission on its own. That, in short, is why all of these texts are in the *Riesencodex*; she and her editors wanted everyone who saw this volume to understand that each of these genres were valuable for her prophetic career. In other words, the *Riesencodex* loudly proclaims that pursuing Genre Diversity was what being a prophet was all about.

Embracing Genre Diversity

But what does Hildegard's approach to Genre Diversity do for us? I'm certainly not suggesting that all medievalists become prophetic polymaths like she was. But, like her, I think we need to more loudly advocate for expressing our expertise about the Middle Ages in formats beyond the monograph, journal article, or even the classroom. Hildegard helps us understand that there are plenty of options out there that can share our knowledge about the Middle Ages just as well as—and, in some cases, *better* than—traditional scholarly publications, because they can create exciting opportunities for audiences who aren't professional scholars.

As a way to make this idea more concrete, I'd like to share a small but illuminating experience of the benefits of Genre Diversity that I had in the winter of 2024. In the preceding fall (2023), the Newberry hosted *Seeing Race Before Race*, a gallery exhibition exploring race-making from the Middle Ages up to 1800 that I had the honour to co-curate. This exhibition was the first exhibition at the Newberry (so far as I know) that presented medieval and early modern books, documents, and visual art from the Newberry collection through the lens of critical race studies. It was, in other words, an opportunity to engage traditional Newberry audiences (which tend to be older and wealthier) in an unfamiliar yet urgent topic as well as audiences (especially communities of colour) who had not previously felt welcome in Newberry spaces or, for that matter, the field of medieval or early modern studies.

With all that in mind, my co-curators and the Exhibition Department at the Newberry were eager to think of as many ways to engage those different audiences as we could. That included public programming, a digital resource, an exhibition video, and a professional development workshop for teachers. But perhaps the most important of these "assets" was an exhibition catalogue co-edited by Dr. Noémie Ndiaye and Dr. Lia Markey, *Seeing Race Before Race: Visual Culture and the Racial Matrix in the Premodern World*, which featured contributions from a wide range of medieval and early modern scholars (including graduate students), curators, and librarians. From the beginning, everyone on our curatorial team agreed that this wasn't going to be your typical academic catalogue; our main goal was accessibility. But in order to get it, we knew we'd have to do more than just ask all our authors to avoid using academic jargon.

Without ever using the term, we turned to Genre Diversity. Alongside the typical features of an exhibition catalogue (analytical essays, item-level descriptions, and *lots* of images), *Seeing Race Before Race* included brief "Notes from the Field" about critical race studies in the respective worlds of libraries, museums, and theatres (41–49, 129–34; 183–88); an interview exploring the connections between premodern critical race studies and Indigenous Studies (217–28); and, one of my personal favourite additions, a glossary of the various technical and field-specific terms used throughout the book (229–34). By adding these decidedly *less*-scholarly genres and formats, we hoped that the catalogue would be able to bring the story of race-making before 1800 to people who didn't already have PhDs in medieval or early modern studies: people like retired professionals, self-proclaimed lifelong learners, activists, and students, especially undergraduates and high schoolers.

The catalogue came out in April 2023, in plenty of time for it to take a prominent spot in the Newberry Bookshop before the show opened the following September. Well before that time, however, the Newberry's incomparable bookshop manager, Jennifer Fastwolf, had been hard at work curating a selection of other books, ephemera, and swag to sell that would fit with the theme of the exhibition. Naturally, that selection included a substantial number of scholarly publications on premodern critical race studies from some of the best and brightest minds in the field: Olivete Otele, Noémie Ndiaye, Cord Whitaker, Jonathan Hsy, and plenty more. I remember the thrill I had walking into the bookshop on the day the exhibition opened and seeing all those titles sharing the same shelf-space. It was exceedingly familiar; in fact, it was exactly the same kind of feeling I get whenever I walked into the exhibition hall at Kalamazoo or the Medieval Academy's annual meeting. Throughout the run of the show, I'd occasionally wander into the bookshop to get that feeling again, and to revel in the fact that so much great work was being made available to Newberry audiences.

A few months after the exhibition closed, we all gathered for a debrief meeting, where we discussed all sorts of data, feedback, and other measurable reactions to the show, including Jennifer's report from the bookshop. There was, thankfully, a lot of good news. She reported hearing "positive feedback" about the show and the books available for sale, and it seemed that "good questions" were being asked, which was what we wanted. Unfortunately, though, none of that translated into robust sales for the majority of her carefully curated shop selections; all the "academic titles" available failed to move the needle with bookstore patrons, and most of the copies ordered for the show were sent back unsold. All the academic titles, that is, except our exhibition catalogue. Unlike the other books, *Seeing Race Before Race* sold "extensively" in the bookshop, to the point that Jennifer had to order more of them halfway into the show's run to meet the demand. This wasn't limited to the Newberry either; the entire first print run of the paperback version of the catalogue sold out before the end of the year, which was pretty remarkable considering it was also available open-access online.

Small-scale though it was, this experience was a ringing endorsement for the benefits of Genre Diversity. The catalogue was and is not, of course, an inherently *better* study of medieval and early modern race than any of the outstanding, award-winning scholarly titles Jennifer collected, but it was, without question, the *least academic-looking thing on that shelf.* When people opened it, they found more than just page after page of careful analysis, elegant academic prose, and extensive notes. Instead, they found multiple familiar formats (Interviews! Notes! Glossaries!), texts that were shorter and more manageable than they might have expected, and lots and lots of beautiful and interesting images to look at. And what's more, since many of those people saw the catalogue *after* visiting the exhibition itself, the book promised something that the other books on display couldn't: the opportunity to hold on to (or learn more about) the experience they had just had engaging with real, honest-to-goodness medieval and early modern books and other objects. That is why the catalogue sold as well as it did.

Now, to be sure, nobody got rich off the success of the *Seeing Race Before Race* catalogue. But still, the fortunes of the Newberry Bookshop in the fall of 2023 have a lot to tell us about how Genre Diversity needs to be enthusiastically celebrated and promoted by medieval studies. For me, the catalogue's popularity confirmed that so-called "non-specialist" audiences are willing to spend their money on studies of medieval culture (or other academic topics), so long as those studies offer enough points of access for them to get into it. As we learned in the Bookshop, it wasn't enough for the academic titles to be prominently displayed for the public or thematically aligned with a successful gallery exhibition: the scholarly publication format (along with the typically high price point) put up too many roadblocks between the customers and the content that they were obviously interested in. The catalogue, on the other hand, offered more opportunities for learning about race in a much more accessible way (and at a much more reasonable price), so it's only natural that many more people were willing to buy it.

That experience taught me that all it takes to elevate Genre Diversity to forefront of medieval studies is to recognize the simple truth that scholarly publications, as good as they are, can't do everything. There are so many exciting, interesting, and urgent lessons and truths in medieval culture that can and will come across more effectively in other ways. And, like Hildegard, we should realize all the ways in which we share our knowledge of the medieval past are part of the same project. That is, sharing medieval content in a YouTube video, comic book, podcast, or humorous T-shirt is a part of the "good work" we do in our monographs and articles, because those genres can do things and engage people in ways that scholarly publications aren't designed to do. What's more, that makes them just as valid options for sharing expertise about medieval culture as monographs are.

That's why I'm convinced that the more we champion Genre Diversity, the stronger our field will become. When that day comes, the exhibition halls at conferences will look a lot different, because they will give just as much pride of place to movies and TV series, comics and cartoons, works of visual art, novels and short story collections, poetry, music albums, and social media channels as they currently do to scholarly publications. When that day comes, I'll feel even better about those halls, because I know what I see there is visible, tangible proof that we, like Hildegard, are doing our job as best as we possibly can.

Chapter 3

HENRY SUSO AND AUDIENCE DEVELOPMENT

The Problem: The General Public Fallacy

Now that we've gotten about halfway through this book, there's something I'd like to get off my chest. It's about one of my pet peeves: two little words that come up often whenever medievalists today talk about public engagement: "General Public." Perhaps you've heard this term before, and maybe you've even used it yourself. For a little while now, medievalists have used it a lot when talking about how to solve the current crisis; if we want to stop the field's inevitable slide into oblivion, so it goes, we need to make our work accessible to the "general public." I've especially noticed these words in grant proposals, book descriptions, and the "about" pages on digital resources, right at the point when the creators discuss what kind of impact they'd like their project to have. Usually, it sounds something like this: "While this book/project/digital resource will be most useful for scholars, it will also appeal to the general public."

Now, you might be wondering, what's the problem with that? Isn't bringing medieval studies out of the academy and into the lives of the "general public" what this whole book is about? It's a fair question, and I do have to say that, on a certain level, the growing presence of the "general public" in medieval studies is a good thing, because it means that, at the very least, more medievalists are taking the challenge of building productive connections with non-academic audiences more seriously than in the past. And yet, that phrase still gets on my nerves; every time I hear a medievalist use it (or any of its relatives like the "general audience" or "general readers") in the context of public engagement, I cringe inside like someone's scratching their nails on chalkboard. The reason why has nothing to do with the intentions of whoever is using the term, which are usually good. Instead, it has to do with the fact that, from a public engagement standpoint, the "general public" isn't nearly as helpful as it sounds. In fact, I think the field's increasing reliance on this term does way more harm than good.

In this chapter, we'll take on this roadblock by exploring all the ways that this deceptive concept is preventing medievalists from developing content that will truly make an impact on any audiences outside of academia.

We'll be able to see that more clearly in comparison with the medieval solution, which generally avoids the temptation to reach *everyone* by focusing on gradually building relationships with much smaller audiences. Finally, I'll explain how I found myself unknowingly following that same medieval approach in the depths of the COVID-19 pandemic, as my department looked to develop digital resources that would help our consortium in a time of great need.

For the most part, when academic medievalists say, "general public" to describe the audience they hope to reach, what they really mean is "anyone who isn't an academic." This sounds like a fine idea—and it is, at least at first—but let's see what happens if we push on that concept just a little bit. Who belongs to the general public? What do they like? How do they prefer to consume their content? If we define our preferred target audience as "not academics," questions like these—which are essential for effectively reaching this "general public"—become impossible to answer, because there are simply too many ways to answer them. The "general public" contains an enormous variety of people who differ wildly in terms of age, race, gender, sexual orientation, personal interests, religion...the list goes on. As if that weren't enough, those demographic categories intersect in a nearly limitless number of combinations, like "white retirees in rural communities," "Black high school students in Chicago," "18–25-year-old males of South Asian descent," "mid-career female investment bankers," and so on.

This is what bugs me about the "general public." From a public engagement perspective, it has so many possible meanings that it really has no meaning at all. As such, it does not actually help us grow the field in the ways we want. On the contrary, I believe it's actually holding us back, in the form of what I call the General Public Fallacy. This roadblock is a trap that lures in well-meaning medievalists who want to save their field with promises of being able to connect with broader audiences outside the academy, but in reality, it saddles them with an overly vague concept of a target audience that obscures all the things you need to know and the work you need to do to reach it successfully. Without this knowledge, medievalists who aim for "the general public" quite often end up producing work (whether in print or online) that looks and sounds a lot like a scholarly publication (there's Genre Dependency again!), only without as many pages, footnotes, and jargon. This kind of work is, to be sure, more accessible than your standard scholarly publication, but it's also rather aimless, not specifically geared towards any one audience in particular. Not surprisingly, these attempts haven't really moved the needle all that much in how audiences outside academia imagine the field.

All that has left us in a situation where it seems that the best we can do is just keep throwing slightly more accessible content at the "general public," hoping that it will somehow convince everyone that medieval studies matters. That's certainly not out of the realm of possibility, considering the number of things (both the good and the ridiculous) that have become cultural phenomena just because someone put them "out there." But the odds of that are slim. By staying on this path, we might get some more non-expert eyes on what our field does, but the impact is still pretty minimal. At best, employing the General Public Fallacy is more like buying a lottery ticket than making a serious attempt to grow new audiences for medieval studies. Because of that, the recent increased effort to reach the "general public" has given us little more than a growing anxiety about why potential audiences and stakeholders outside of academia still don't seem to understand why what we do is important.

So, does this mean that we should just give up trying to reach non-academic audiences? Certainly not, we just need to do it the right way, and that starts by opening our eyes to what it really takes to make our work appealing and interesting outside the so-called ivory tower. And make no mistake, there *is* a right way to do this. In fact, it's going on all around us in the marketing and communications departments found in basically any business or institution in the private and public sectors.[1] And as my colleague Dr. Rebecca L. Fall has taught me, it's even happening in some corners of academia, especially in the fields of theatre and media studies, whose practitioners' livelihood depends on building and sustaining audiences who will buy tickets to their performances.[2] For these professionals, details matter. Rather than putting things out there and hoping for the best, they want to know everything they can about smaller subgroups within the "general public": who they are, what they do, their likes, their dislikes, and so on. This knowledge, in turn, helps them develop strategies and initiatives to which those audiences are more likely to respond positively. If we really want our work to mean something outside the academy, we need to get this knowledge for ourselves. But can we even do that without hiring a marketing firm? I think so. After all, that's precisely what our medieval predecessors did.

---

1 Palmer, *Introduction to Marketing.*

2 Cf. Hall, "Encoding and Decoding in the Television Discourse"; Sedgman, *The Reasonable Audience* and "Audience Experience in an Anti-expert Age"; Bennett, ed., *Theatre Audiences*; Eagleton, "Phenomenology, Hermeneutics, and Reception Theory"; and Hohendahl, "Introduction to Reception Aesthetics."

The Medieval Solution: Audience Development

You might think that something like the General Public Fallacy might be appealing for intellectuals in medieval Europe, considering the fact that they lived and worked in a society that was divided (by law, no less!) into church (*ecclesia*) and not-church (*saeculum*). But, as we've already seen with Peter Damian and Hildegard, those spheres were never as sharply divided in medieval Europe as they might seem to us. More importantly, though, elite intellectuals knew perfectly well that both the ecclesiastical and secular spheres contained within them a plethora of smaller, more narrowly-defined audiences that differed significantly in terms of education, wealth, status, geography, language, custom, gender, age, devotion, and more. Getting their message out to such a diverse group of publics would take a lot more than just wishful thinking. To be specific, it took something that I call Audience Development.

Broadly speaking, Audience Development is about filling in all the details that the General Public Fallacy glosses over. That is, it's about learning everything you need to know in order to, as much as possible, ensure that a particular audience will be receptive to whatever content you share with them. Unlike the General Public Fallacy, Audience Development offers no shortcuts; it's probably best understood as a process, one that takes time, effort, and patience to see all the way through. It's also much smaller in scale, usually focusing on a single, well-defined audience instead of everything at once. Medieval intellectuals were ready for all that, however, thanks to their training. Classical rhetoric, which was ultimately based on the context of a legal case tried before a jury, taught them that a good orator always needed to focus on a specific audience—understanding who they were, what they liked and didn't like, and so on—if they were going to effectively convince them of anything.[3] Professional intellectuals in the Middle Ages took that to heart, and most of them probably would have agreed with our old friend Peter Damian's comment that, "An arrow is fired more truly if a target is set up for it" (Ep. 1, 1:67). That ability to isolate and cultivate smaller audiences became even more important as medieval society grew steadily more complex and diverse after the twelfth century, which created ever more potential audiences that needed to be served.

This was no doubt a major challenge, but the evidence suggests that medieval intellectuals were up to the task. We know that not just from their

---

3 Cf. Cicero, *De inventione*, ed. Greco, 100, and Pseudo-Cicero, *Rhetorica ad Herennium*, ed Müller, bk. 4, chap. 15, §22; bk. 4, chap. 29, §39.

own work, but from how much time, money, land, and goods were donated to the Latin Church by laypeople of all kinds. Now certainly the church's ability to provide access to salvation had a lot to do with all that money rolling in, but I think it's important to note that, on the whole, intellectuals didn't take that for granted. As we've already seen, they spent an enormous amount of time and effort reaching out to people beyond the academic elite by writing to them, preaching to them, administering sacraments to them, making books for them, visiting them, teaching them, and lots more besides. They put in all this effort because they understood that the material support they needed wouldn't come unless they were willing to put in the work to get it.

For us, that work can be hard to see a lot of the time; medieval intellectuals had internalized Audience Development so well that they saw no need to spell it out. But, as usual, there were some elite intellectuals who were more open about how they built productive connections with certain audiences, and, accordingly, their work shows all the steps of the Audience Development process particularly clearly. In this chapter, we'll talk about one of the most enthusiastic medieval audience developers I know, one who spent decades growing and nurturing a relationship with an audience that ended up making a much broader impact than he initially expected. Through his example (a very appropriate term, as we'll see), you will get a better sense of everything that goes into Audience Development...including how it can make *your own* work better.

The Model: Henry Suso

Our model for this chapter is Henry Suso (1295?–1366), a Dominican friar who lived and worked in what is now southern Germany and Switzerland. He lived in tumultuous times, to say the least. The first two-thirds of the fourteenth century saw, among other things, theological controversies, dramatic political instability caused by infighting between the Holy Roman Emperor and the papacy and, oh, a cataclysmic plague that devastated everything in its path. Faced with all that, many people throughout Europe quite understandably became interested in turning away from the apparently crumbling world to develop their inner spiritual lives.[4] That interest fit into a longer tradition of medieval people (especially women) trying their hand at living a holy life *outside* of traditional religious institutions. In the fourteenth-century German lands, this movement gained so many adherents and spawned

---

4 Cf. Tobin, "Introduction," 14–15, and Kieckhefer, *Unquiet Souls*.

so much religious cultural production (texts, images, practices, and so on) that later scholars gave it a special name: *die deutsche Mystik*, or "the German mysticism." Led by highly-trained intellectuals (mostly from the Dominican order), this movement was marked by a general desire to surrender one's self to the divine or striving for as much spiritual perfection as possible. It was *exceedingly* popular with pretty much everyone in the German lands. Men and women, vowed religious and laypeople, highly-educated scholars and amateur novices, and more tried to leave their troubled world behind by seeking the Godhead in a variety of ways: contemplating divine mysteries, reading devotional literature, listening to sermons, commissioning art, and lots more.[5]

Henry Suso is probably best known for being one of the leading male figures of *die deutsche Mystik*.[6] Like many in his time, Suso was deeply interested in obtaining a special, intimate relationship with God, which, in broad strokes, came from detaching oneself from the cares and worries of the world to (hopefully) experience a close relationship with the divine, or at the very least, an understanding of what such a relationship would be like (6).[7] He liked to describe himself as the "Servant of Eternal Wisdom," and was famous among his contemporaries for his command of mystical theology, his many religious visions, and his seemingly superhuman feats of asceticism. His writings were well-known in his own day, especially in southern Germany and Switzerland, and went on to influence the devotional lives of professional academics as well as ordinary laypeople for centuries after his death.[8]

Suso was without question a product of elite intellectual culture; as a young man he was one of the few chosen to study at the famous Dominican *studium generale* at Köln, an elite finishing school dedicated to creating highly-skilled professionals who would guide the intellectual and spiritual development of future generations of the Order of Preachers.[9] Suso proved to be an excellent teacher, and not just of his fellow Dominicans; he was widely recognized—and sought out—by religious and secular audiences

5 Cf. McGinn, *The Harvest of Mysticism*, and Haas, *Sermo mysticus*.

6 Cf. Filthaut, ed., *Heinrich Seuse*; McGinn, *The Harvest of Mysticism*, 195–239; and Enders, *Gelassenheit und Abgeschiedenheit*.

7 This and all other Suso references in this chapter indicate the page in Heinrich Bihlmeyer's critical edition of Suso's German works.

8 Bihlmeyer, "Einleitung," 3*. On Suso's works cf. Tobin, "Introduction," 26–51, and Ruh and Haas, "Seuse, Heinrich, OP."

9 Cf. Tobin, "Introduction," 21–22, and Ruh, *Die Mystik des deutschen Predigerordens*.

alike for his ability to effectively teach profound theological ideas and guide devotional activities. But despite his credentials, Suso didn't think of himself as a university master or a profound mystical authority. "To me," he later wrote, "it appears that I am [God's] cart-driver, and, with my robe rolled up, I drive into puddles to drag people out of the deep muck of their sinful lives and bring them to beautiful things" (385).

This, obviously, paints quite a different picture from what we might expect from an elite intellectual in medieval Europe. And, for his part, Suso preferred not to be thought of that way; he deliberately turned his back on the way theology was learned and taught in the schools in favour of something more effective with less-educated audiences. In the first place, that meant doing most of his writing and teaching in German rather than Latin. It also meant avoiding complex argumentation and dense commentary in favour of teaching in what he described as "a model-making fashion" (*mit gebildener wise*) (3). Yet, unlike most other authors of his day, his writings were deeply personal, expressing his own strong emotions and physical experiences as he explored theological and mystical ideas.[10] This helped him develop a style that brought his work to life for his readers by incorporating dialogues, personal anecdotes, and plenty of borrowed language and structure from popular vernacular literature like courtly romances.[11]

Medievalists today have a lot to learn from this "cart driver." In particular, Suso is ideal for helping us understand how we too can roll up our sleeves and do the work necessary to develop enthusiastic and supportive audiences outside the academy. Instead of putting his ideas out there in the hopes that someone, somewhere would pick up on them, Suso met his target audience where they were, so he could lead them to where he believed they should go. And he could only do *that* through his strong commitment to Audience Development, which (luckily for us) he made sure to talk about in detail in his surviving work. Thanks to that, we know that Suso succeeded not because he knew a lot of theology, read a lot of literature, or put himself through an extraordinary amount of suffering, but because he knew what he had to do to find, understand, and, ultimately, *serve* his audiences in the ways that they needed.

---

10 Bihlmeyer, "Einleitung," 148*.

11 Cf. Ruh and Haas, "Seuse, Heinrich, OP," 1124; Molinelli-Stein, "Seuse als Schriftsteller"; and McGinn, *Harvest of Mysticism*, 299–365.

Henry Suso and His Audience

The best source we have for Suso's Audience Development is *The Exemplar*, a collection of his most important vernacular works that he revised in the few years before his death. It contains "four good books" (*vier gůtú bůchlú*): *The Life of the Servant*, *The Little Book of Eternal Wisdom*, *The Little Book of Truth*, and *The Little Book of Letters* (3). The title of this collection was a deliberate choice: he wanted all four books to "provide for the good-hearted a clear path to heavenly truth, and for the right-minded the true path to the highest kind of blessedness" (6). But who was supposed to follow that model? Suso himself didn't give a clear answer; all he says in the prologue is that "it was God's good will that it be shared far and wide with all good-hearted people who, with the right mindset and an almost-painful yearning, desired to have it" (6).

If it sounds to you like Suso is treading very near to General Public Fallacy territory, you're not alone. He certainly does leave the door open for thinking that anyone (who can understand German, anyway) could be the target audience for *The Exemplar*. However, Suso scholars are quite certain that they know exactly who his original target audience was: Dominican nuns. Their confidence comes from a variety of internal and external evidence. In terms of numbers, Dominican sisters are mentioned directly or indirectly more than any other (human) figure throughout the different books in the *Exemplar*, a clear sign that he expected them to be reading it. The constant use of images throughout the surviving manuscripts of the work—including a series of illustrations almost certainly developed with Suso's involvement—is also a vital clue, as that practice was important for the instruction of nuns in medieval Germany.[12] Then there are the manuscripts; of the fifteen complete copies of *The Exemplar* to survive from the Middle Ages, ten of them were created for use in Dominican convents, and the quality of those manuscripts gives us some indication of how the nuns felt about Suso.[13] Take for instance, a beautiful copy of *The Exemplar* now in the collection of the Herzog August Bibliothek in Wolfenbüttel that was made for an unknown Dominican convent (possibly in Nürnberg) in 1473.[14] Everything about the book—its large size; its fine wooden, leather-bound covers; over one hundred large initials decorated by colourful pigments and

---

12 Hamburger, "The Use of Images."

13 Blumrich, "Die Überlieferung der deutschen Schriften Heinrich Seuses."

14 Henry Suso, *Heinrich Susos Buch genannt der Süse*, Wolfenbüttel, Herzog August Bibliothek, Cod. Guelf. 78.5 Aug. 2°, fol. 38r.

Figure 3. Portrait of Henry Suso from a fifteenth-century copy of the *Exemplar*. Wolfenbüttel, Herzog August Bibliothek, Cod. Guelf. 78.5 Aug. 2°, fol. 38r. Available online http://diglib.hab.de/?db=mss&list=ms&id=78-5-aug-2f. Courtesy of the Herzog August Bibliothek.

goldleaf; and nearly two dozen rich illustrations that sometimes take up a full page—was clearly meant to impress. I can confirm that this book still stops people dead in their tracks in the reading room, a clear sign of the high regard the sisters who commissioned it must have had for its author, even more than a century after his death (Fig. 3).

Clearly, the relationship between Suso and Dominican nuns in the southern German lands was something special. Indeed, to hear Suso tell it, it's impossible to imagine the *Exemplar* existing at all without them, or one in particular, at least. Her name was Elsbeth Stagel, a member of the convent of Töss in Winterthur (present-day Switzerland), and Suso considered her his most important "spiritual daughter."[15] So important, in fact, that in the prologue to the *Exemplar*, Suso rather remarkably claims that half of his "four good books," *The Life of the Servant* and *The Little Book of Letters*, owe their existence to her. Of the two, the story of the *Life*'s creation is the more dramatic, and, as we'll see, far more useful for thinking about Audience Development.

Suso tells us the *Life* was originally a set of notes Stagel had secretly compiled from a series of conversations with him about his past experiences, especially the ones that related to his special relationship with Eternal Wisdom. When Suso found out what she'd done, he was horrified, and demanded she hand all her notes over so he could destroy them. Before he could burn everything, though, a "heavenly message from God" commanded him to save the rest, most of which, he asserted, remained "as she wrote it with her own hand," albeit with some "good teachings" added by Suso later on (7–8). This is a remarkable claim of collaborative authorship, to be sure, and scholars have debated how seriously to take it for decades, with all agreeing that we will probably never know for certain how much, if any, of the *Life* as we have it was Stagel's work.[16] We *do*, however, know two things: 1) Suso wanted his contemporary readers to believe that the *Life* was, at the very least, co-authored by a Dominican nun and 2) those same medieval readers had no reason to think otherwise.

This makes the *Life* the most important text for understanding Suso's approach to Audience Development, because it has the most to say about his relationship with the primary public he served. As such, it has all the details about what he had to do to build and maintain that audience, so it will be our focus for the remainder of this chapter. Before getting into that, however,

---

15 On Stagel's life, see *Verfasserlexikon*, ed. Wachinger (1995), 219–26.

16 Tobin, "Henry Suso and Elsbeth Stagel."

we need to talk about some, shall we say, quirks about this text. Despite its name, the *Life* should not be taken as a totally accurate, autobiographical account of Suso's own life; it is perhaps better thought of as an "auto-hagiography" that was meant to teach important lessons about sanctity and devotion to fourteenth-century audiences.[17] In fact, Suso deliberately avoided using the first person at all in the work; referring to himself (or, if you like, the literary figure standing in for himself) as "the Servant" (*der Diener*), most likely to make it easier for his future readers to see themselves on the path of progression to spiritual understanding that the text lays out.[18]

So...is this authorship situation a problem? Does it mean that the Audience Development model we find in this text is all just a product of Suso's imagination, and didn't ever really happen? And does *that* mean that Suso's example won't help us overcome the General Public Fallacy? I don't think so. Whether Suso himself actually followed through on any part of the process we'll talk about below (and, for what it's worth, I'm convinced he did), it doesn't make it any less valuable for our purposes. After all, Suso meant for the *Life* to teach people how to do things by giving them useful, legible models to follow, which is precisely what we're looking for in this book.[19] In other words, the whole point of the text was to lay out all the practices and assumptions that experts often leave unsaid, but that beginners like us need spelled out in plan detail. That brings us back to Stagel (or, if you like, the literary figure standing in for Stagel), and Suso's claim of authorship for her. Whether she actually wrote any part of the *Life* or not, medieval readers of the text would have seen in her proof that Dominican sisters—again, *Suso's target audience*—played a major role in shaping his elite, intellectual production. In that sense, the story of Stagel's authorship is basically the desired outcome of Audience Development—an enthusiastic and capable audience member who can appreciate, engage with, and even participate in a particular field. The rest of the text, then, explains the meticulous, gradual, and intensive method Suso put into practice to make that happen. And all it takes are five easy steps!

---

17 Kieckhefer, *Unquiet Souls*, 6.

18 Cf. McGinn, *The Harvest of Mysticism*, 196, and Willliams-Krapp, "Henry Suso's Vita."

19 Bernhardt, *Figur im Vollzug*.

Step 1: Commitment

Trite as it may sound, the first step in Audience Development according to Suso is to really, truly *want* to do it. He began his process by thinking—constantly and with great effort—about what audiences were out there and how they might respond to his work. That wasn't particularly common in the fourteenth century; Suso himself noticed a dip in the piety and dedication within the Dominican Order in his day, so he probably knew more than a few friars who didn't feel it was worth their time to think about other audiences.[20] Indeed, it wasn't inevitable that Suso would either; he began his serious spiritual life at eighteen when he resolved to make "a constant effort to earn an enduring experience of a loving union with eternal Wisdom," which he did initially by keeping himself apart from other people as much as he could to focus on his own progress (11). But after doing that for a long time, "he was charged by God through all kinds of revelations to strive now for the salvation of his neighbours" (63). From then on, he could no longer enjoy the company of his heavenly beloved unless he was thinking about how to serve other people.

Divine commands aside, Suso had other reasons to care about audiences. One was a painful personal experience. In 1330, he was summoned before a chapter of the Dominican order to answer accusations that his writings (most likely *The Little Book of Truth* and maybe some others) contained heretical teachings, and though he was not condemned, the humiliation that came from what he felt were misreadings of his work stayed with him for the rest of his life.[21] Another reason was his preferred form of spiritual life; enduring a seemingly endless series of physical, mental, and spiritual sufferings to attain true detachment. For him, these acts were just the necessary first step on a path towards a union with Eternal Wisdom, but he worried that external observers would be more likely to see them as "sharp thorns that pierce all the way through flesh and bone," which would discourage them from pursuing the spiritual life on their own (90).

With all this in his mind, it's no surprise that Suso cared deeply about audiences and how they responded to his work throughout his career. That concern comes out clearly in the *Life*, which is filled with anecdotes about individuals and groups giving him (mostly positive) feedback on his teachings, writings, and way of life. Some of those reviews even came directly from God. For example, a Dominican nun named Anna told Suso about mul-

20 Bihlmeyer, "Einleitung," 96*–100*.

21 Cf. Tobin, "Introduction," 23 and 33, and Künzle, "Einführung," 30.

tiple visions in which God confirmed his pastoral work and dedication to suffering were indeed helping bring other people to salvation (63–64). References like these were more than just confirmations that Suso was doing good work; they were a reminder that his audiences were not abstractions, but real, living people who could, based on their reactions, have a decisive impact on the successful attainment of his spiritual goals.

That was certainly on his mind as he was compiling the *Exemplar*. In the prologue, we learn that Suso's original plan for the work was to lock it away until after his death, when it would (we must assume) be "put out there" to what one could rightly call a "general public." In the end, however, he decided to scrap that plan and disseminate the book himself, because:

> It could well have been the case that, after his death, the book would have found its way to men who were tepid or fallen away from God's grace, who would have made no effort to share it with those desiring to praise God, sending it into oblivion having done no good at all. It could also have happened, that it would have first come to those who are blind to the truth or had spiteful minds, who out of the wickedness in their hearts would hide it away, as has often happened before (5).

This confirms that Suso's desire for Audience Development came from his concern for his neighbours; he was extremely worried about the harm that would be done—to his work, his reputation, and, most importantly, to the spiritual fates of his neighbours—if it ended up before the wrong audiences. That was more likely to happen if he just released *The Exemplar* to a "general public" and hoped for the best, so he chose to take the surer thing and put in the effort to get his work in front of the right people first. Turns out, he chose wisely.

Step 2: Identification

After all that careful thinking about what audiences he could serve, it was time for Suso to choose one. But why did Suso settle on the Dominican nuns as his target audience? One might say that the decision was made for him, since the spiritual direction of the sisters had been (by papal command, no less) the responsibility of the friars since the thirteenth century.[22] However, this didn't mean that Suso would inevitably choose to work mainly in Dominican convents. The sisters were far from the only audience Suso would have served in his capacity as a friar, nor were they the only ones to merit a mention in his works. Indeed, the *Life* shows Suso interacting with

22 Tobin, "Introduction," 16 and 24.

people across the social spectrum: wealthy noblewomen, poor travellers, other Dominican friars, townspeople, a knight and his squire, and even a self-acknowledged murderer and his girlfriend. Any one of these audiences (well, probably not the murderer) could have been the audience he chose to develop a close relationship with, so what was it about the nuns that drew his attention?

For one thing, there were an awful lot of them. The Dominican province of Teutonia, which included southwestern Germany and Switzerland, contained more convents (sixty-five) of the order than any other province in Europe, so there was a real need for friars to take up the charge of working with them.[23] Another selling point was that the sisters tended to be highly competent for spiritual instruction; most of them came from noble or urban families, and were usually able to read and write, at least in German, even before they entered the convents.[24] Because of that, the sisters could become active participants in devotional work, even to the point of making their own texts. Multiple convents created so-called "sister books" (*Schwesternbücher*), which gathered together autobiographies of members of the convent that functioned as devotional models for future generations.[25] Elsbeth Stagel herself took part in compiling one such book for her community of Töss, most likely in collaboration with her sisters, which Suso himself called "a very good book" (*ein vil gůt bůch*) (97).[26] Finally, Dominican sisters were enthusiastic participants in *die deutsche Mystik*, having already developed a fairly sophisticated practice of mysticism without the assistance of the friars.[27] As such, it is safe to assume that many of them possessed the same confidence in their religious abilities that Stagel expressed to Suso in the early days of their relationship: "My desire is...to live a holy life, and for that I have the courage to properly and rightly pursue it...be it through...suffering, death, or whatever it is...whatever painful thing you have the courage to tell me to do, I will do it with the help of God's strength" (98).

These factors combined to make the Dominican sisters the ideal audience for Suso's brand of spiritual cart-driving: they had a clear need for his services, they were competent enough to pursue a mystical spiritual life,

23 Grundmann, *Religiöse Bewegungen*, 313–14.

24 Folini, *Katharinental und Töss*, 339.

25 Tipka, "Subjekt und Text."

26 On Stagel's *Schwesternbuch*, see *Verfasserlexikon*, ed. Wachinger (1995), 223–24, and Grubmüller, "Die Viten der Schwestern von Töß und Elsbeth Stagel."

27 Peters, *Religiöse Erfahrung als literarisches Faktum*.

they were untrained enough that they still required guidance from a professional like him, and they had the conviction necessary to endure the long road towards "supreme happiness" with the Godhead. Suso clearly had a lot to offer an audience like this, but, just as important, he also understood that the sisters had a lot to offer *him*. As active students, interlocutors, and even devotional partners, Dominican nuns themselves could exert a significant, positive influence on the religious life and work of their spiritual directors.[28] This certainly was the case for Suso and Stagel; near the end of the *Life*, he remarked that "I have never had anyone who could, with such tenacious effort and devotion to God, help me complete my books, as you did" (109). This settled it. If Suso wanted the world to get the most out of his intellectual and spiritual expertise, the Dominican nuns of Teutonia had to be his main audience.

Step 3: Relationship-Building

His choice made, Suso then had to turn to actually creating a relationship with the Dominican nuns. This was a big challenge; just because the sisters *seemed* like the ideal audience for him to prioritize did not automatically make them a *receptive* one. That was only likely to happen if he was able to build a proper relationship with them, which required more than wishful thinking from afar. As with a great many relationships even today, the key was for him to *be there*. From the sources we have, it's clear that Suso made sure he was a regular physical presence for his spiritual daughters in all the ways a friar was allowed to be: he celebrated mass with them, heard their confessions, preached sermons before them, answered their questions, talked about readings, and provided other general spiritual guidance.[29] But all of this was just a base-level form of engagement; more would be required to get the kind mutually-beneficial *spiritual* relationship he was looking for.

For Suso, that meant the intimate conversation, a type of interaction that suited his emotional and personal approach to spiritual direction very well indeed. Appropriately enough, we see conversations happening constantly in the *Life*, with human and divine interlocutors alike.[30] The dialogue format had a long history in Christian religious thought, of course, but Suso's use of it was unique in the sense that his dialogues seemed like conversations actual humans would have. Alongside quotations from theological authori-

28 Grundmann, "Die Frauen und die Literatur im Mittelalter."

29 Michel, "Heinrich Seuse als Diener," 282.

30 Enders, *Gelassenheit*, 223–45.

ties and citations from Scripture, a chat between Suso and his spiritual children featured poetry, music, jokes, wordplay, references to shared memories, stories, and romance tropes, among other things. At the same time, Suso knew how to approach conversations with a high level of emotional intelligence, especially when the sisters were distraught. For instance, he recalled a time when a number of women (some of them Dominican nuns) who were held "captive" by fear and other troubles came to him for help. Before doing or saying anything else, "he openly wept with them in their fear and distress" and comforted them, a display of genuine empathy that helped the women eventually break free from their troubles after their conversation (116–17).

Even with all this, however, relationship-building was not always easy, and Suso often had to show persistence and resourcefulness to get through to a tougher audience. But once again, the conversation was key to his success. One of the best examples of this from the *Life* involved a beautiful young Dominican nun who had not, shall we say, fully committed to her vocation, being more interested in hanging out with her noble friends than living an austere, focused spiritual life. For precisely that reason, she had no interest talking to Suso, and avoided him at all costs whenever he came around her convent. When he finally did approach her and "tactfully" tried to start a conversation, the nun angrily shut him down and drove him off. Humiliated but not defeated, Suso developed a new plan straight out of a romantic comedy: asking one of the nun's friends to make up some excuse for her to go into the guest house where he was staying so he could talk to her alone. Once he did, Suso turned on the emotion, sighing deeply before making an extremely flattering pitch (just to give you an idea, here's how it started: "Ah me, my beautiful, gentle maiden, chosen by God, how long will you let your lovely, beautiful body and your fine, tender heart belong to the devil's cruelties?"). Immediately following their conversation, the nun dismissed her noble friends from her company and committed herself to seeking true detachment (135–8).

Step 4: Listening

As deeply meaningful (and even enjoyable) as these intimate spiritual relationships could be, though, Suso understood that they were only another step on the way towards developing his audience. The next step was to get a clear sense of what the Dominican sisters actually wanted to get out of the relationship for themselves, since that would guarantee his work would have the positive impact he hoped for. It was probably natural for Suso to think about what people wanted from him, since the *Life* includes a great many anecdotes of people, sometimes complete strangers, coming to him out of the blue to ask for some kind of spiritual service. However, it's important to note that very few of those anecdotes have the same level of detail as the requests from nuns. These often appear as full-bodied conversations, in which the sisters express their wants and needs in their own voices. Not surprisingly, no sister does this more frequently or more in-depth than Stagel, and her exchanges with Suso are probably the best evidence we have for what a good listener he was.

As Suso described, Stagel had demonstrated a strong sense of initiative well before she knew him. She was like "the hard-working bees" in that she "wrote down whatever she was able to find that could lead her and others to practice holy virtues" (96). She carried those strong, intentional work habits into her relationship with Suso, always coming prepared with specific questions and clearly-articulated goals for what she wanted to get from his expertise at any given time. Indeed, she decided to reach out to him in the first place because she had heard about some "high-falutin' and sagacious ideas" that interested her, and she somewhat brazenly requested that Suso "write her something about these aforementioned ideas without any kind of background" (97).

Though Suso (as we'll see in a bit) declined to do precisely that, this first exchange set the tone for the rest of their spiritual relationship, as Stagel continued to request specific services like receiving consolation at a tough time, learning the difference between false and real detachment, or an explanation of the Trinity (114, 158, 191). As if that weren't specific enough, she was not shy about telling him *how* she wanted to learn from him, either. In Suso's telling, all the rhetorical and pedagogical strategies we see in the *Exemplar*—Suso's own experiences, "models for imitation" (*bildgebender glichnus*), and brief, uncomplicated summaries of complex ideas—were at some point specifically requested by Stagel, so that Suso's teachings would, as she put it, "last longer in [her] unhealthy mind" (99, 190–91).

It might be easy to characterize Stagel's assertiveness here as a token of Suso's esteem for her, were it not for *where* in the *Life* they show up. We begin to see these details in chapter 33, which scholars agree marks the beginning of a second part of the text. At this point Suso replaces himself (or the Servant) as the main focus of the narrative with Stagel, who goes on to follow the ideal model of spiritual progression laid out in the first part.[31] It's here, in other words, that Suso expects the *Life*'s readers to start actively

31 Hamburger, "Medieval Self-Fashioning."

imitating the things that Stagel does, which means that he wanted *all* of his readers, but especially Dominican nuns, to also be prepared to tell their spiritual directors exactly what they wanted from them.

Step 5: Serving

By this point, Suso had put in so much work to develop his target audience that it might be easy to forget that he hadn't actually shared any expertise yet. This was, of course, no accident; after the previous four steps, he wasn't in a position to do so successfully until this point. Now he knew for certain that Stagel and other Dominican nuns had the following interests: pursuing a "holy life" based on "true detachment," thinking about lofty intellectual concepts discussed by elite thinkers, and performing acts of asceticism. What's more, he also knew that they preferred to learn about those subjects through intimate conversations, letter exchanges, and models they could visualize and imitate. Armed with this knowledge, he knew exactly what parts of his expertise to share with them *and* how to do so in a way the nuns were sure to like.

Often, Suso simply gave the nuns precisely what they asked for. Usually that meant providing them with information about certain ascetic practices that would help them on their way towards mystical understanding, many of which he had used himself when he was a beginner. One example was a morning greeting he would customarily give to Eternal Wisdom; the *Life* included a full description of this greeting; what words he said, what he was physically doing (a physical prostration) when he delivered it, the short prayer he said afterwards, and even a reference to one of his other works (*The Little Book of Letters*) where that prayer could also be found (18). The sisters also asked for many religious texts, which was a bit more complicated, but Suso did his best to accommodate them. The trick was to give them enough so that they felt they got what they wanted, but not so much that anybody would get in trouble. For example, because the sisters were keen on learning from Scripture, Suso filled his works with Scripture quotations (and their accompanying explanations) as much as possible, so that they could justifiably say that Suso gave them a stronger command of the Bible than they'd had before.[32] At other times, Suso created new texts for the sisters by excerpting or summarizing longer, more difficult ones. He sent both kinds to Stagel at various times, like a copy of sayings of the Desert Fathers and excerpts from theological writings about obtaining unity with

---

32 Michel, "Heinrich Seuse als Diener," 286–87.

the Godhead, which reads much more like a miniature treatise than the rest of the *Life* (104–7, 184).

Suso also shaped how he expressed his knowledge based on the nuns' pedagogical wishes. When he did finally get around to discussing the "high-falutin'" theological concepts Stagel originally requested, he made sure to do so gradually and in an orderly fashion as she had asked him to do, sending her a concise, thoroughly sign-posted "good breakdown" (*gůten underscheide*) of three kinds of detachment that "you can understand from now on" (*du nu fúrbaz merken*) (163). And of course, as we've seen, Suso gave Stagel and the other nuns all of the "visible models" (both textual and visual) they could handle from Scripture, the lives of the saints, and his own experience (35–36). But plenty of elite intellectuals could heap up examples; Suso's were different because he used his literary gifts to bring them to life, making them more like the intimate, in-person conversations everyone enjoyed so much throughout the *Life*. For instance, he filled a description of how he performed the stations of the cross with intense, physical details about what happened when he "met" Mary along the way so that the nuns could also see her tears, hear her sighs, and witness the sorrow on her face as if they were standing before her (35–36).

Of course, any good teacher knows it is not a good idea to *always* give students exactly what they want or expect, and sometimes Suso had to serve his favourite audience by telling them "no." In fact, that was how his spiritual instruction of Stagel began. When she first approached him to get expert-level instruction on some "sagacious" theological ideas without the proper instruction first, alarm bells went off for Suso. He knew well that many others (including seasoned professional scholars with more formal education and training than Stagel would ever get) had taken those ideas and run with them to questionable places that led to confusion, controversy, and, sometimes, heresy.[33] That, however, put him in a difficult spot: if he flatly refused her request, she may well have just gone to some other spiritual director with less scruples than Suso or, perhaps worse from his perspective, she would stop trying to pursue divine understanding at all. Either of those things would have to count as an Audience Development failure, so Suso avoided them both with a well-crafted response that acknowledged she was doing the right thing: "You recently told me about some lofty ideas…which you handled very delicately, as you should." Then he explained why he could not grant her request: "You seem like you are still a young and inexperienced

33 Lerner, *The Heresy of the Free Spirit.*

nun." Finally, he provided her with information on how she could eventually get what she wanted: "it's better for you to know how to start at the beginning...[with] ascetic practices and good examples of the holy saints" (98–99). In this way, Suso made sure that, even though he didn't give Stagel what she specifically requested, he was still providing her with the service she had asked for.

To be sure, Suso was not always successful in his interactions, even with Dominican nuns. Overall, though, between the evidence from the *Life*, the broad circulation of manuscript copies of his writings, and the popular cult that began after he died, I think we can say with confidence that the man knew how to develop an audience. So how did he do it? First, he started with the determination that bringing his work to other audiences was essential. Next, he thought carefully about what specific audience would allow him to have the biggest impact, both on the audience and on his own work. Then, he steadily built a relationship with that audience, which gave him a solid sense of what that audience's interests and preferred content formats were. That then helped him shape his expertise into a product that was sure to find a positive reception. The bottom line is this: Suso was able to serve Dominican nuns like Elsbeth Stagel so effectively because he knew them so well—who they were, what they could do, what they were interested in, and how they liked to learn. At the same time, his "spiritual daughters" also knew *him*, because he had worked so hard to be present with them and share his own feelings as much as possible. All of this created a powerful sense of mutual trust that benefited all parties, including, lest we forget, *The Exemplar* itself, which, thanks to Suso's tireless dedication to Audience Development, had the right audience to bring it into the world.

Embracing the Smaller Audience

It is, I hope, clear how *radically* different the model of Audience Development we find in Henry Suso's *The Life of the Servant* is from the General Public Fallacy. Rather than trying to aim his work at the entire non-professional world at once, Suso started with a very clearly-defined audience (Dominican nuns) and worked diligently to build a productive and trusting relationship with them that, in turn, shaped how he shared his expertise with them. And in the end, everybody won: sisters like Stagel got the spiritual guidance they were looking for, and Suso was able to bring more people up from the "mire" into a holy life. On top of that, the strength of the relationship he built with his core audience was a key factor in spreading his expertise to other audiences as well. As the sisters discussed, shared, and copied Suso's works, more and more people (visitors, donors, family members, and so on) came into contact with them, helping to grow his reputation and create connections with different audiences that came to appreciate his work. In the end, it's mostly thanks to the sisters that Suso became the most widely-read of the major figures of *die deutsche Mystik* during the Middle Ages.[34] In other words, Suso "went viral" in the way that a lot of medievalists today hope to do, but only because he had steadily and meticulously developed a smaller, more narrowly-defined audience first.

To be clear, Audience Development is not always nice and linear like this. In fact, it wasn't even that way for Suso. There were starts and stops, and plenty of "two steps forward, one step back" going on, and that would be true today, too. Audience Development is, as it was for Suso, a constantly ongoing, flexible process that can start at different levels, sometimes skip a step or two, repeat the same step multiple times, or start over completely. What I've done here is order all of these different aspects of Audience Development into a progressive sequence (in a "model-making fashion," you might say) so that you can visualize the whole process, from first wanting to bring your work to others to successfully doing so. Depending on who you are, what your abilities are, and what you want your work to do, your experience of this process may be very different. But, trust me, it can work.

I saw this firsthand back in the late spring of 2020, when, along with everyone else, the Center for Renaissance Studies at the Newberry was trying to figure out what to do about the first full academic year in the age of COVID. That meant knowing what was going on with our consortium, because serving the needs of the faculty and graduate students in our consortium is literally the main reason why the Center was founded in the first place. Not only that, we knew that we had a degree of flexibility that our colleagues at universities didn't, so we always try to make sure to use that to get our constituents what they need. So, that spring, our director, Dr. Lia Markey, diligently reached out to friends and colleagues in the academy to get a sense of how we could help them in the year to come. What she learned was that everyone, anticipating (correctly, as it turned out) that Zoom would be a major factor in however the year went, was looking for digital things to do with their students. In particular, they were looking for YouTube videos that were short (around 5 minutes), included a lot of images, and were based on actual medieval or early modern objects to use in their (likely virtual) classes. So, we all decided that was exactly what we would make.

---

34 McGinn, *Harvest of Mysticism*, 195.

I volunteered to try and put together a prototype that would help us learn whether or not this was something we could actually pull off.

This turned out to be *much* easier than I expected. Within the week, I had developed, practiced, and recorded a presentation on Gregory of Tours' account of the impact of plague in the city of Marseilles in 588. That recording became the first entry in a series of videos called *Learning from Premodern Plagues*, which you can now find on the Newberry's official YouTube channel.[35] When the fall term came, just as we had hoped, our faculty and graduate students reported using the videos right away in their classrooms, and we were glad to hear they were working exactly as our instructors had hoped. But then, to our surprise, we learned that other audiences, including many outside of academia, were also watching, enjoying, and learning from the videos, as well. As of July 7, 2025, the videos have collectively received over twenty-three thousand views and counting.

I remember being impressed at how easily my *Learning from Premodern Plagues* video came together, but, upon further reflection, it was not all that surprising. The experience was so seamless and effective because we knew exactly what to do. That knowledge came from the fact that we knew our audience so well, thanks to the hard work we had put into getting to know them and understanding what they wanted over a long period of time. When I sat down to start planning out the proof-of-concept recording, I already had detailed knowledge of who the intended audience was (university instructors and their students), what that audience needed (digital videos), and precisely what format it should have (short, image-based). All of this helped me to resist falling down rabbit holes, getting lost in needless details, or getting too much into my own head. Lia's advance research had already laid out all the dots, all we had to do was connect them. And once we did, we very quickly found that other people beyond our original audience wanted to join in.

Though none of us realized it at the time, the story of creating *Learning from Premodern Plagues* followed Henry Suso's model for Audience Development almost to the letter, which is why I'm confident that the model can work for other medievalists, too. It will, of course, not be that easy; as Suso knew, developing an audience properly takes a lot of effort, dedication, and persistence. No question, it sure would be easier if some medievalist could produce one book, TikTok video, or podcast that would immediately con-

35 https://youtube.com/playlist?list=PLA6qRZ3gfQFbmaJ-aaaM_OZdVU2ohF1hA&feature=shared.

vince the mythical "general public" to love medieval studies. After all, there is a reason so many people still play the lottery. But, given the crisis we're facing, our field doesn't need lottery tickets, it needs sure things. And Audience Development can get us those sure things if we're willing to put in the work.

I know that sounds daunting. One of the biggest challenges of Audience Development is that it can take a long time before we can see visible evidence that it's working. That, in part, is why the General Public Fallacy is so enticing; it would be much better to just get everyone on board with medieval studies at once, right? So, I want to finish this chapter with one way that Audience Development makes the work of building productive connections with audiences easier: it gives us permission to *start small.* That is to say, there's no need for us to try and reach the biggest possible audience right away; instead, like Suso, we should try to get to that point by reaching as many more narrowly-defined audiences as we can. If more medievalists commit themselves to developing small audiences as Suso did, before you know it, we'll have collectively added a pretty large audience to the fold. To put it another way, the smaller audiences we're able to develop, the bigger medieval studies' base of social and financial support becomes. At a certain point, we should be able to see that in (hopefully) more undergraduate enrollments, more graduate students, and more non-academic members in organizations like the Medieval Academy. And if we can keep that up, administrators and funders eventually will *have* to take notice.

So, by all means, please do understand how important it is to make your work accessible to an audience that isn't academic, but don't let that understanding fall into the General Public Fallacy when you do. Instead, be like Henry Suso and hop out of your cart, roll up your robe, and go pull a well-defined audience out of the mud and into what's medieval.

Chapter 4

NEWBERRY INC. 1699 AND AUDIENCE EMPOWERMENT

The Problem: Gatekeeping

Who gets to be a "medievalist"? This might come across as an odd question for many professional medievalists, especially if they're in a graduate program. I assume that their answer would be the same as mine was while I was working towards my PhD: someone who has completed (or at least pursued) advanced study of the Middle Ages at a university in a humanities discipline of some kind. It seemed like a logical answer at the time; after all, every person I had ever known who called themselves a "medievalist" either had a PhD already or, like me, was on their way to getting one. In fact, I didn't even think I'd earned the right to refer to myself as "a medievalist" until I got into my doctoral program; before that, I was just a "history major who liked medieval history."

I don't think I'm the only one who reads some kind of professionalization into the word "medievalist." It seems to me that plenty of people outside the field think so, as well. So, too, does the Oxford English Dictionary, which has this as the primary definition of the word: "An expert in or student of medieval history, culture, etc." Right after that, though, we find something a bit different: "Also: a person who practises or is sympathetic to medievalism in art, religion, etc." Hmm. This definition seems to suggest that someone *without* an advanced degree, that is, someone who just "likes medieval things," could also call themselves a "medievalist." Do you agree? Which of these definitions do you think is the *better* definition?

If someone were to do a survey of just this question, my guess is that a majority of respondents would go with the first option in the OED. And if you asked that question just to professional medievalists, I think that majority would be even bigger. In fact, it seems to me that people in the field have an even more stringent definition of that term than the OED does. Based on my experience, I think the field's working definition of a "medievalist" looks like this: "An expert in or student of medieval history, culture, etc. that is formally affiliated with an institution of higher learning." While I doubt that many (if any) professional medievalists would admit to thinking that, the huge numbers of former PhDs in medieval studies working outside a university who report feeling isolated or shut out from the field by their former mentors and colleagues is proof enough that it's plenty common.[1] And that's what I want to talk about in this last analytic chapter. The idea that only a trained expert in a medieval topic who's working in (or, like me at the time of this writing, adjacent to) academia gets to be a medievalist comes from our final, and perhaps most challenging, structural roadblock: Gatekeeping.

In this chapter, we'll talk about how to get around this most difficult obstacle for effective public engagement. For starters, we'll go into some more detail about the dangerous way in which Gatekeeping subtly encourages medievalists to keep non-specialists from fully engaging the field. Next, I'll explain how medieval intellectuals managed to avoid this roadblock by actively encouraging non-experts to do the sort of intellectual work the pros did. Finally, I'll tell you about how I finally left Gatekeeping aside after unwittingly helping to develop the most virally-engaging digital resource in the history of the Newberry Library.

It is in no way an exaggeration to say that Gatekeeping is absolutely *poisonous* to effective public engagement. After all, it's hard to make a positive connection with an audience if a door always gets slammed in that audience's face. To be clear, I'm not suggesting that gaining expertise in medieval studies is a bad thing; I think it's essential that people take the time to learn languages, engage with scholarship, and do archival research so they can produce new knowledge about the Middle Ages. All that expert knowledge becomes the foundation for any successful public engagement we as a field can possibly do. Having said that, if we give the impression (through our words and/or our actions) that only the experts doing this work can count as medievalists, it becomes much, *much* harder for any of that public engagement to work. Even if we understand our work as a public service, develop and value creative ways to share our expertise, and go through all the hard work of developing a receptive audience, Gatekeeping has the power to shut it all down. The reason why is simple: if you want an audience to really engage with and support your group, at some point, *they need to feel like they're a part of that group.* That is, the people doing all the public engagement (professional medievalists) have to make their target audiences feel welcomed, valued, and appreciated within the field. Gatekeeping doesn't want to allow any of that; it prefers to keep any potential outside stakeholders just as they currently are: passive, outside observers who simply appreciate the field from afar.

---

1 Caccipuoti and Keohane-Burbidge, eds., *Independent Scholars Meet the World.*

It wasn't always this way, of course. Back in the nineteenth century you would have found a lot of medievalists according to the second definition from OED: these were people without PhDs who wrote books about medieval topics, composed poetry and novels inspired by medieval themes, went to go see medieval manuscripts in academic libraries, incorporated medieval architecture into their houses, and so on.[2] In other words, there once were lots of people without advanced humanities degrees who were willing to devote their time, money, and energy to engaging deeply with medieval content. In fact, they got so excited about it that it freaked professional scholars out, driving them to create the "scientific" field of academic medieval studies as a way separate the "real" medievalists from the mere amateurs.[3] But even then, non-academic medievalists didn't go away overnight; as Patrick Geary noted over a decade ago, in its earliest days the Medieval Academy of America (founded in 1925) included "great philologists" (i.e., the pros) alongside "architects, businessmen, and educated amateurs."[4]

Of course, by 2009, those non-expert medievalists in the Academy had all but vanished, and the situation seems even worse now. For that, we mainly have Gatekeeping to blame. But that's not the worst of it; I hold Gatekeeping responsible for a host of other problems plaguing the field, including (but not limited to) the crushing sense of imposter syndrome afflicting so many graduate students;[5] its consistent focus on Europe;[6] the persistently privileged, white, and male nature of the field and its published work;[7] and the profound sense of abandonment and isolation that comes when medievalists can't get a permanent position in academia.[8] So, if we want to save the field, Gatekeeping has to go. We have to find a way to maintain the high standards that lead to reliable and useful knowledge-making about the Middle Ages—that is to say, *not* what white supremacists are doing—at the same time as we make space for non-experts to do the same. Even within academia, this is not an entirely new idea. Indeed, there already is an entire subfield of history—public history—that is devoted to bringing people without PhDs into the work of making history, by giving them the necessary skills, resources,

2 D'Arcens, ed., *The Cambridge Companion to Medievalism.*

3 Biddick, *The Shock of Medievalism.*

4 Geary, "What Happened to Latin?," 872.

5 Feenstra et al, "Contextualizing the Imposter 'Syndrome.'"

6 Lomuto, ed., "The Medieval Undone."

7 Ramos, "Confronting Whiteness."

8 Caccipuoti and Keohane-Burbidge, "Introduction," 17.

and, most importantly, a sense of co-ownership in the process.[9] To this point, though, public history hasn't had much room for fields like medieval studies, in large part because the field is still predominantly an American one, where medieval history is in no way "local." Nevertheless, there have already been calls for professional medievalists to validate and learn from amateurs,[10] but creating that space within medieval studies remains a really tough task, which is why I think this structural roadblock is going to be the most difficult one for us to overcome. But, trust me, it can be done. In fact, it already *has* been done, all the way back in medieval Europe.

The Medieval Solution: Audience Empowerment

The antidote to this structural roadblock is something I like to call Audience Empowerment, which I define as inviting non-expert audiences to *participate* in expert work and providing them with the necessary training or tools to do so successfully. We don't really have anything like this in medieval studies today, but it was all over elite intellectual culture in the Middle Ages. Certainly, professional medieval intellectuals also knew all about Gatekeeping, and were very happy to practice it, especially when it came to anything having to do with the church and its doctrine, reading the Bible, or fraternizing with non-Christian cultures.

And yet, there's plenty of evidence to show that, when it got right down to it, medieval intellectuals understood that they *needed* the help of non-experts if they were going to actually make a difference with their expertise. The church, after all, was not technically "of the world" anyway, so if they were going to make any impact in it (as their intellectual culture demanded that they do), they would have to have the support and assistance of laypeople to do it.[11] And we've seen a lot of that evidence already in this book. To give just a few examples, Peter Damian tried to make nobles like Adelaide of Turin and Godfrey of Tuscany feel like they were serving God just as much as he was; Hildegard needed people of every social station to take up monastic virtues to get the world into its proper state; and Henry Suso understood that he needed the validation and perspective of his many different "spiritual children" to feel like he was doing his job.

But it's important to note that in these collaborations, medieval intellectuals didn't think of these lay participants as just "the help." Instead, non-

9 Boyle, "Envisioning New Economic Models."

10 Dinshaw, *How Soon Is Now?*

11 Howe, "The Nobility's Reform."

professionals could be full-fledged *participants* and even *collaborators* in the kind of work that elite intellectuals were doing. Alongside giving monetary and political support, non-experts could also do scaled-down versions of the same things the pros did, such as explain basic doctrines, actively participate in the liturgy, or encourage others to live an upright life.[12] But perhaps most importantly, whenever non-experts did those types of things well, professional intellectuals wanted them to know that they were not just pale imitations of the "real" experts. Peter Damian, for example, once told a layman who read a sermon on Damian's behalf that "it is understood that any Christian is, through the grace of Christ, also a priest, and so is fully worthy of announcing his mighty works to the world." (Ep. 145, 3:528).

This is what it looks like when an expert completely validates the work a non-expert does to support their field. Damian wasn't suggesting here that Cencius could administer sacraments or anything like that, but he was clear that "any Christian" was fully capable of helping intellectuals further the divine mission of the church. Even if others didn't put it in quite those terms, there is plenty of evidence Damian wasn't the only medieval intellectual who felt that way. Audience Empowerment explains why Peter Damian seemed confident his correspondents would be able to use the spiritual resources he sent them, why Hildegard encouraged nobles and laypeople to practice the monastic virtues, and why Henry Suso wrote in German and cared so much about the validation and interest he received from his non-expert audiences. In short, intellectuals realized that they could sit in a quiet cell like Sad Ovid and write the most mind-blowing, brilliant study on divine truths of all time, but without non-experts out there learning those truths and putting them into practice, it wouldn't make a lick of difference. The field of medieval studies today needs the same mentality.

In this final analytical chapter, we'll take a closer look at this vitally important medieval solution. But it's going to be a bit different this time. I could line up more medieval intellectuals talking about how valuable the work of their non-expert collaborators was, but I don't think that gets to the heart of the matter in the best way. If we really want to get a handle on Audience Empowerment, we should be looking at the uninitiated audiences that medieval intellectuals were empowering. In the next sections, that's exactly what we'll do, thanks to a unique manuscript witness from the late fifteenth century, which will give us a better sense of how audiences outside

12 Van Engen, *Sisters and Brothers of the Common Life.*

the intellectual elite were trained to participate in that intellectual culture, and, more importantly, how they made that training work for them.

The Model: The Owner of Newberry Inc. 1699

Our model for this chapter is a bit more complicated than the previous ones. This time, our model comes from a book: a late medieval hybrid book (that is, one that includes both printed and manuscript material) that now resides at the Newberry, where it's catalogued as Inc. 1699.[13] Or, rather, our model is the individual who made this book (or had it made for them) in the last decade or so of the fifteenth century. Compared to the authors in the other chapters, there's a lot that I don't know about this person. I couldn't tell you for certain what their name was, where they lived, what they did for a living, when they were born and died, or anything like that. As you'll see, I'm pretty sure that they were German and definitely not a member of the intellectual elite, but that's about it. And yet, despite all this uncertainty, I'm positive that we couldn't ask for a better model to understand Audience Empowerment.

We know that by the time we get to the fifteenth century, elite intellectuals like Damian, Hildegard, and Suso had been actively engaging non-expert audiences for centuries. But for a long time, we couldn't find much hard evidence for any participation by these "ordinary" Christians; all we really had to go on were the texts produced by the elite intellectuals themselves. That started to change in the twelfth century, when we begin to see more manuscripts being made specifically for laypeople's use, including some in the vernacular. Elite intellectuals were behind a lot of these manuscripts, especially the ones that helped laypeople do spiritual work like chanting the Psalter or praying the monastic hours. In the early days, the majority of these manuscripts were commissioned by wealthy noble patrons, but things really started to open up in the fourteenth century, when the increasing availability of paper as a writing support, the rising number of professional scribes working for ecclesiastical and secular institutions who had time for private commissions, and the growing levels of vernacular literacy through-

13 Thomas of Kempen, *Ein ware nachuolgung Cristi* (Augsburg: Anton Sorg, 1486), Chicago, The Newberry Library, Inc. 1699, fols. 198r–230v. My evidence for this chapter comes from both the printed and manuscript portions of this book, so you'll find two different citation methods. References to the printed book point to the original foliation in Roman numerals (e.g., fol. XVIII), while manuscript citations use the modern foliation in Arabic numerals (e.g., fol. 223v).

out Europe made it possible for individuals of modest income and social status to acquire and use books.[14]

By the fifteenth century, then, we finally have widespread, visible evidence for what uninitiated laypeople actually got out of all the public engagement elite intellectuals had been sharing with them for the previous millennium. The agency of these ordinary laypeople shines all the way through these manuscripts, whether they commissioned them from a professional scribe, acquired them second-hand, or made them themselves.[15] So, even though we don't know many biographical details about the owner of Inc. 1699, their book can tell us a lot about 1) what sorts of things a layperson without advanced training took from elite intellectual culture and 2) how they put what they learned to use for their own spiritual benefit.

At the time it was made, there wouldn't have been anything especially remarkable about Inc. 1699. Hybrid books like this were quite common around the end of the fifteenth century, and could be found in the collections of wealthy, elite patrons and intellectuals as well as laypeople of middling means and status.[16] Moreover, the contents of the volume—the first German edition of Thomas of Kempen's wildly popular *Imitatio Christi* and a manuscript miscellany of commentaries, tracts, prayers, and poetry in the vernacular—fit with what we would expect from a compilation of late medieval devotional literature. This makes it an even *better* source for Audience Empowerment, because it means that the approaches and goals we find in here would have been pretty common throughout medieval Europe.

So what do we know about our anonymous model? By using the evidence in the book, there are some things we can be pretty confident (if not completely sure) about. For starters, we can guess that they didn't belong to the intellectual elite, since the entire volume (both printed and manuscript) is entirely in German. At the same time, this owner wasn't completely uneducated; they had obviously learned to read and write in the vernacular, maybe because it was necessary for their job.[17] We can also safely assume they weren't super-wealthy; the modest quality of the book's paper, ink, binding and the general absence of decoration suggest the owner saved whatever costs they could to afford to buy the book.[18] Finally, we can safely

14 Cf. Kwakkel, "A New Type of Book," and Parkes, "The Literacy of the Laity."

15 Johnston and Van Dussen, eds., *The Medieval Manuscript Book*.

16 McKitterick, *Print, Manuscript and the Search for Order*, 48–52.

17 Parkes, "The Literacy of the Laity," 557–60.

18 Fletcher, "Customising Mindset," 43–46.

guess that the owner lived in some kind of medieval city—most likely Augsburg—where you would be more likely to find literate laypeople who were interested in (and capable of) owning books.[19]

But the most important thing Inc. 1699 gives us the confidence to say is this: its owner was an *active* reader. There is all manner of physical evidence throughout the book that it didn't spend its life closed on a shelf or locked in a trunk. Marginal notations, a manicule, and pastedowns show how the owner directly engaged with all the texts inside. Smudges, stains, tears, and thumbprints are signs that the owner worked carefully through the entire volume, rather than focusing on a few sections. Finally, faint reddish stains and a few spots of dried wax drippings are clues that the owner used this book while eating or working, day and night. Based on all this evidence, we can say for certain that Inc. 1699 belonged to a person who was willing to spend their money, time, and resources to enthusiastically and regularly participate in medieval intellectual culture. In other words, the owner of Inc. 1699 is a perfect representative of *exactly* the sort of lay audience medieval intellectuals had been interested in reaching since at least the eleventh century.

Elite Intellectual Culture in Inc. 1699

Let's start by looking at what the content of the devotional miscellany can tell us about how well Inc. 1699's owner knew what was going on in elite intellectual culture. Altogether, the manuscript includes eleven separate texts and/or coherent groups of texts, all of which appear to have been chosen carefully and deliberately for this particular manuscript (Table 1).[20]

As we look over this list, we can already see some clear connections to elite intellectual culture. One of the first things that jumps out is that a lot of names here would have been very familiar to, say, professors of theology at the time: Bernard of Clairvaux, Thomas Aquinas, Albert the Great, and Augustine of Hippo. Though we know that some of these are misattributions, Inc. 1699's owner didn't; as far as they were concerned, their book contained legitimate works by some of medieval intellectual culture's heaviest hitters. Another striking observation is the impressive diversity of genres—commentary, small tract, prayers, poetry, hagiography, and even a plain old list of facts—which shows that the owner was interested in a wide range of intellectual work, ranging from basic things like litur-

19 Fletcher, "Customising Mindset," 54–55.

20 Fletcher, "Customising Mindset," 43.

Table 1. Contents of the devotional manuscript miscellany in Chicago, The Newberry Library, Inc. 1699, fols. 198r–230v.

Commentary on the *Salve Regina*	fols. 198r–201r
Pseudo-Thomas Aquinas, *De divinis moribus* (excerpt in German)	fols. 210r–218v
Prayers to the Five Wounds of Christ	fols. 218v–220r
Poem on Dying Well	fols. 221r–222v
Versified Quotations from Church Fathers (authors unknown, Albert the Great, Augustine, Bernard of Clairvaux)	fol. 223r–223v
A "Mirror" on the Virtues	fols. 223v–224r
St. Bernard's Eight Psalm Verses	fols. 224r–226r
Secular *Priameln*	fols. 226v–229v
Numerological Table of Life Expectancies	fol. 229v
Spiritual *Priameln*	fol. 230r–230v

gical practice (the *Salve regina* commentary) all the way up to scholastic theology (*De divinis moribus*). Just based on these quick observations, then, I think we can safely say that a non-expert layperson like the owner of Inc. 1699 was interested in pretty much any content they could get from professional religious thinkers.

But, having said that, we shouldn't assume that this was just a random collection. All but one of its texts (and we'll get to that one in a bit) was copied out by a professional scribe who was working from at least one exemplar, which suggests that each of them was *deliberately* chosen.[21] That was probably a harder chore than we might think; by the late fifteenth century, there was a staggering amount of devotional and theological material available to non-expert lay readers in all kinds of formats and genres, from written texts and oral traditions to physical practices and visual art. Given what we know about medieval manuscripts, it's safe to assume that the owner themselves would have been heavily involved in deciding what to include.[22] And rather than put all their eggs in one basket, so to speak, the owner of Inc. 1699, as many lay readers and bookmakers did, chose to make themselves a miscellaneous compilation of shorter texts that came from different genres but could be combined into a cohesive work that was uniquely meaningful to them.[23]

21 Johnston, *Scribes and Readers*.

22 Johnston and Van Dussen, "Introduction."

23 Hanna, "Vernacularity and Miscelleneity," 49.

When we put all that together with the physical evidence of use in the book that I mentioned earlier, we're left with a really important takeaway: Inc. 1699 wasn't just a book, it was a *tool*. Its untrained lay owner had invested money and time in acquiring it so they could use it to do something that would be spiritually beneficial for them. Remember how we talked above about intellectuals making a difference in people's lives? Well, dear reader, here's the proof: Inc. 1699 can help us understand how someone without any expert-level knowledge used the work of elite medieval intellectuals to guide some aspect of their life.

Putting Intellectual Culture to Work in Inc. 1699

It sure would have been great if the owner of Inc. 1699 had left a detailed note somewhere telling us exactly why they wanted to have all these different texts in their manuscript. But, since they didn't, we'll have to figure out what this manuscript did for them another way. Our first clue about this is actually in the *other* book in Inc. 1699: the first printed edition of Thomas of Kempen's *Imitatio Christi*. This devotional work was already a runaway success in 1486, helping readers across Latin Christendom achieve "the conversion of one's life and a complete destruction of the desire for pleasurable things that make one a true Religious" (fol. XVIIIv).[24] The secret sauce for the *Imitatio*'s success was its lack of detail. The four relatively short books in the work all contain useful tips on how to successfully pursue the "inner life," but are also purposefully vague about how exactly to do it. So, for example, Thomas encouraged his readers to "Never be idle; either write or read, pray or do some useful work for the benefit of others," but didn't give any suggestions about what things to read, what prayers to pray, or what works one might do (fol. XXIIv). This ended up being a good thing, because it meant that individual readers were able to fill in those details with whatever made the most sense for their particular interests. In a way, you might say that the *Imitatio* invited its readers to make the text work for them. I think this is exactly what manuscript in Inc. 1699 was supposed to do. Every one of those texts was there to help the owner do something that made it easier for them to follow the "inner life" amidst the hustle and bustle of urban life.[25]

It can be a tricky thing to try to make meaning out of a miscellany, especially if you don't have specific notes from the compiler. Luckily for us, I think there is something in this manuscript that can help us out: a collec-

24 Neddermeyer, "*Radix studii et speculum vitae*."

25 Fletcher, "Customising Mindset," 54–59.

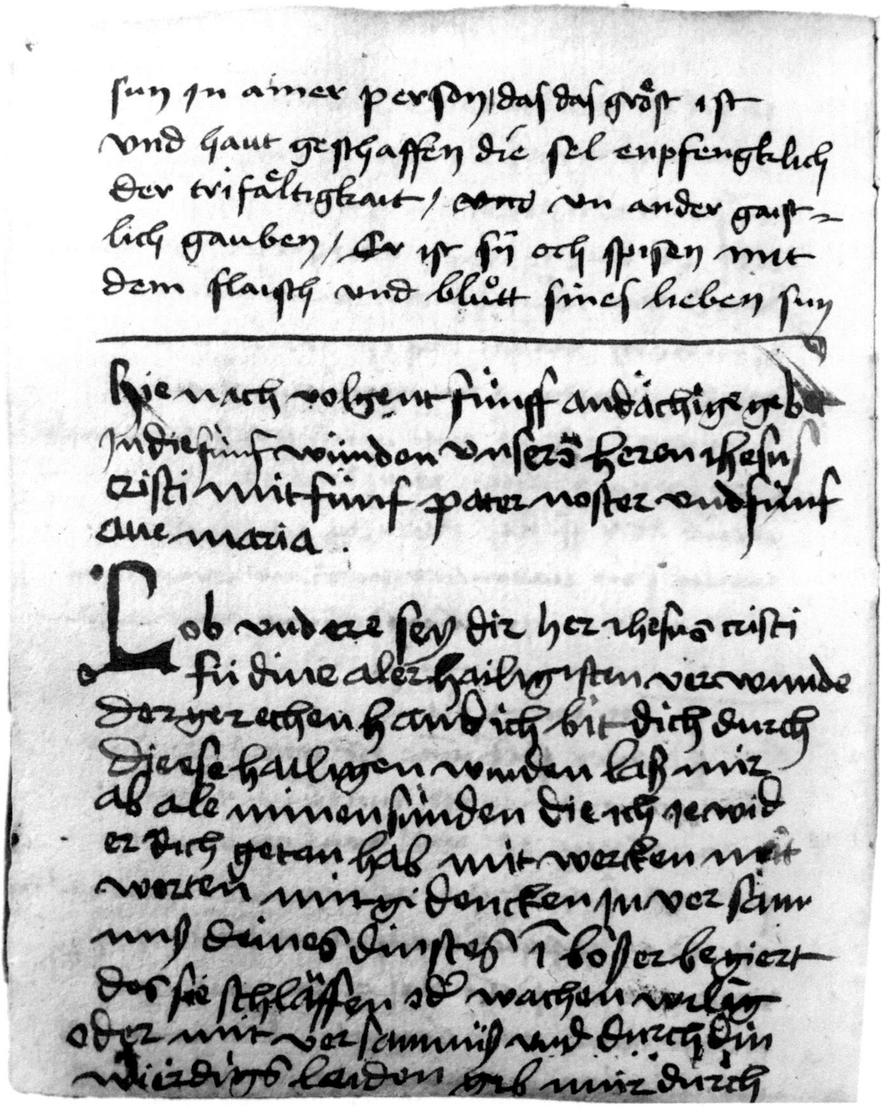

Figure 4. Beginning of the devotion on the five wounds of Christ. Chicago, The Newberry Library, Inc. 1699, fol. 218v. Photograph by author. Courtesy of the Newberry Library.

tion of "five devout prayers" (*fünf andächige gebet*) to the Five Wounds of Christ that's copied on a few folios in the middle of the manuscript (fols. 218v–220r) (Fig. 4). The reason this text jumps out at me is how, well, *messy* it looks. Compared to the steady, consistent hand in all the other manuscript texts, this devotion was copied out by someone who let their lines wander up and down, smudged a bunch of words at the end of lines, and left almost no margins. This text, in short, was definitely *not* copied by a professional scribe, and for us, that's *great* news. It gets even better when you factor in the location. Folios 218v–220r round out the first quire of the manuscript, which contains the *Salve regina* commentary and the *De divinis moribus*. After the professional scribe had finished copying these texts, about one and a half folios remained blank. This naturally created an exciting opportunity for the book's owner, who could fill that space with anything that they wanted.[26] Messy as it is, it seems to me that the devotion to the five wounds was copied in a fifteenth-century hand, which means there's a very good possibility that this text was put there by the original owner of Inc. 1699 themselves. If that's true, then this scruffy little devotion can tell us a lot about what sorts of spiritual activities the owner felt would help them live the "inner life." In other words, the "five good prayers" are like a key to help us decode the purpose of the rest of the manuscript, which can help us see how an ordinary layperson made elite intellectual culture work for them. In what follows, we'll use it to isolate a few general rules that determined how the owner of Inc. 1699 selected the most useful texts from the mountain of available religious material in the fifteenth century.

Rule 1: Keep it Short

The first principle is obvious just by looking at the text: it's pretty short, taking up just a little more than one full folio of a manuscript that was already pretty small to begin with. This makes a lot of sense for a non-expert reader, who wouldn't have had the time to carefully work through a long, dense treatment of anything. The owner seemed to take that approach to heart, making this already-brief text even smaller, so to speak, by subdividing it into five subsections that include a prayer to each of the five wounds Christ received at the crucifixion: the right hand, left hand, right foot, left foot, and side wound (respectively). But the owner didn't stop there. Even those subdivided prayers could be broken down still further into three distinct sections: an introduction, the prayer itself, and a cue to recite "five Lord's Prayers and five Hail Marys" (fol. 218v). In short (sorry), what we have here is the kind of text that a busy layperson in a medieval city could use to master a set of prayers that was easy to use and easy to memorize. When it came to non-experts, in other words, it seems that shorter was better.

---

26 Knight, "Organizing Manuscript and Print," 90.

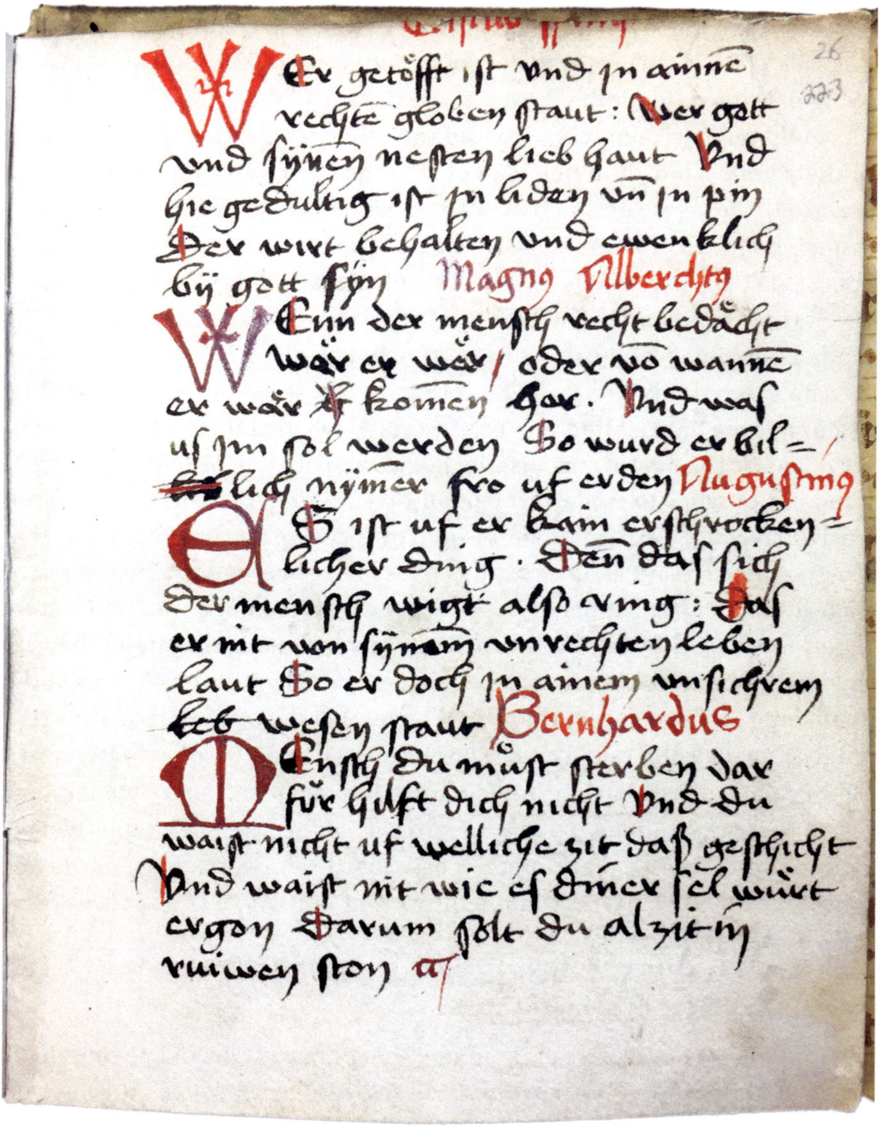
Wer getöfft ist vnd jn ainne
rechte globen staut: Wer gott
vnd synen nesten lieb haut Vnd
hie geduldig ist jn liden vn jn pin
Der wirt behalten vnd ewenklich
by gott syn Magnus Albertus
Wenn der mensch recht bedächt
wär er wär / oder wo wanne
er wär her komen har. Vnd was
uf jm sol werden So wurd er bil-
lich nymer fro uf erden Augustinus
Es ist uf er kain erschrocken-
licher ding. Den das sich
der mensch wigt also ring: das
er nit von synem vnrechten leben
laut So er doch jn ainem vnsichrem
leb wesen staut Bernhardus
Mensch du must sterben dar
für hilft dich nicht Vnd du
waist nicht uf welliche zit daß geschicht
Vnd waist nit wie es diner sel würt
ergon Darum solt du alzit jn
ruiwen ston

Figure 5. Versified, translated, and adapted quotations from elite religious thinkers. Chicago, The Newberry Library, Inc. 1699, fol. 223r. Photograph by author. Courtesy of the Newberry Library.

That rule holds up in the rest of the manuscript, as well. Not a single one of the other texts could be called "long" in any real sense. Some of them, like the "mirror meant for rich and poor, great and small, noble-born, young and old," are little more than a series of short lists describing various virtues, such as "Six virtues adorn a nobleman with the fear of God: Mercy, Humility,

Honesty, Love of Righteousness, Clemency" (fol. 223v). Knowing what virtues to look for in various members of society was pretty useful for someone trying to lead an "inner life," and these texts laid all that out in a format that you could memorize quickly. Most of the other texts have a bit more flesh on their bones, but the same idea of condensing a lot of information into bite-sized packages shows up everywhere. Just before those short lists, for example, comes a pretty impressive feat of brevity: a four-pack of quotations from some truly prodigious medieval theologians—Albert the Great, Augustine of Hippo, and Bernard of Clairvaux (and a fourth name, almost certainly another elite intellectual, that's been trimmed off) (fol. 223r).

The three thinkers named here (Fig. 5) are some of the most prolific authors of the entire Middle Ages, especially when you factor in the number of works (like in this manuscript) that were attributed to them. It could take a lot of work to wade through all that writing, but this page offered the owner easier access to their wisdom by focusing on some key ideas that were condensed and re-imagined as five- to six-line poems. Even the two longest texts in the manuscript, the *Salve Regina* commentary and the *De divinis moribus* translation, try to keep things short by breaking the text down into smaller sections organized by individual words or phrases in the commentary or straight-up chapters (*capiteln*) in the tract. We even see that subdivision idea play out in much shorter texts, like the account of Bernard's eight Psalm verses, which is broken down into eight sections (one for each verse) that are, stop me if you've heard this before, subdivided into eight sections with rubrics marking the particular Psalm verse (e.g., *das ander verß*) followed by a corresponding prayer on that verse (*Das gebet uf den andern verß*) (fol. 224v).

Rule 2: Keep Your Eyes on the Prize

The *Imitatio* was pretty clear about one thing: if you want to live the "inner life," you better figure out how to avoid the secular world as much as you can. Filled with all sorts of distractions, temptations, and annoyances, staying too involved with anything on this earth was a surefire way to put yourself in spiritual danger.[27] And the best way to avoid that, it seems, is to remember that the world is a very, very, *very* bad place. Each of the "five good prayers" definitely got that memo, hammering home the sad state of the reader's earthly existence and encouraging them to reach for heaven instead. The first prayer to the right hand, for example, asks God to "for-

27 Thomas of Kempen, *The Imitation of Christ*, 73.

give me all of the sins I have ever committed against you in deed, word, and thought, and make it so that I, who otherwise wish to be asleep in sin, will wake to become united to your service" (fol. 218v). The prayer to the wound on the right foot emphasizes the end times, asking "that you will, in your divine will, wish to protect me, your unworthy servant, day and night; and that you will mercifully heal all the unworthiness in my body and soul; and... take my soul to you on the Day of Judgment and lead me into Your eternal joy" (fol. 219v).

Not surprisingly, we find that same idea popping up all the time in practically every other text in Inc. 1699. For instance, the versified quotation from Albert the Great says, "If a man rightly considers who he is, or where he comes from and will return to, and what will become of him, he would never be happy on Earth" (fol. 223r). Taking this idea to the next level is a "good poem on the death and dying of Man" that immediately follows the Five Wounds prayers (fol. 221r). Fitting seamlessly into the long tradition of popular devotional literature on dying well, this poem helps the owner look to eternal life by doubling down on the frightening and disgusting fallenness of anything in the earthly one, through the words of a damned soul directed to the living. "For now," the damned soul laments, "God wants to destroy your body like mine, so that you are no longer a person, but become food for frogs, snakes, and worms; the same thing will happen to all of you, so I want to remind you that the pain of hell should lead you to look to God" (fol. 222v). The very last text in the manuscript, a religious *Priamel* (a type of poem in the vernacular), takes a less-graphic approach to the same idea, but still may as well be a condensed version of the entire *Imitatio*: "Keep the love of God in your heart completely," it says, "and in the depths of your soul sweetly / and with all of your might resolutely / serve Him with full effort truly. / Proclaim the Word of God loudly / *Languish through this world fully*" (fol. 230v, my emphasis).

Rule 3: Use Your Skills

Since the *Imitatio* is light on details, the manuscript texts take the opposite approach, by giving specific instructions for what the reader should do when using them. The prayers to the Five Wounds are, as we saw, extremely practical; part of the reason they're subdivided so much is so that the owner can learn how to do them easily. But it's also important to note how much action there is even in such a brief text. The best evidence for that is the "five Pater Nosters and five Ave Marias" that were mentioned in the text's title, which, as we've seen, are duly present at the end of each individual prayer with the phrase *Pater Noster Ave Maria.* The full texts of those prayers aren't written out here, but that's not really a surprise; by the end of the fifteenth century (and probably well before), any devout, practicing member of the Latin Church should have been able to say both of them from memory without much trouble. This is a big deal, because it means that the owner would need to pull something else out of their devotional toolbox, as it were, to get the most spiritual benefit out of this text. These "five good prayers," then, weren't just an opportunity to learn some new devotional material, they were also an opportunity to practice other devotional skills that would help them meet their spiritual goals. It was, in other words, a chance to learn something new while improving something familiar.

Most of the other texts in the manuscript also encourage the owner to sharpen their skills while learning new material. The description of Bernard's eight psalm verses, for example, takes a similar approach as the Five Wounds prayers by appending a prayer to each of the eight verses. However, instead of basic liturgy, these prayers help the owner sharpen their mastery of the Bible itself, because they re-use the very words of the just-quoted Psalm. Take, for example, the fourth verse (Psalm 38:5) "O Lord, grant that I may know the number of my days and how many there are, so that I know what is wanting for me" is followed by this prayer: "Almighty God of gods, be merciful to me, a sinner, and *show me the number of my days and how many there are so that I might know what is wanting for me*" (fol. 225r, my emphasis).

An even more interesting example of adding practical actions to devotional texts is found right at the start, in the *Salve regina* commentary. The *Salve regina* was probably the most popular Marian antiphon by the later Middle Ages, and was often sung at the last monastic hour of the day, Compline.[28] Now, for a song that is supposed to be sung right before bedtime, there sure is a lot of action going on in this commentary. Here's how it begins: "As soon as you have said 'Salve, we greet you,'" it advises, "*immediately leap backwards* into the humility of the great worthiness of the Mother of God and say, 'O you most holy Lady of all the saints, have mercy on me'" (fol. 198r, my emphasis). Instructions like this show up all throughout this text, which makes it clear that actual physical participation is essential for understanding what the commentary says about the antiphon's words. One of my favourite examples of this comes in a later section that talks about the phrase "we cry to you" (*Schrÿend wür*), because the commentary liter-

28 *New Catholic Encyclopedia*, 631.

ally puts a scream (*Eÿa*) into the speaker's mouth, inviting them to really perform this verse (fol. 207v). In that, the text is quite different from other vernacular commentaries on the poem, which tend to simply translate and briefly comment on what the Latin text means.[29] But here, in Inc. 1699, it's the action that counted, because this is what would build up the owner's devotional skills in the way that they wanted.

So, in the end, how did the owner of Inc. 1699 make elite intellectual culture work for them? I think it's pretty clear that they went into the whole process knowing exactly *how* they were going to learn most effectively—through short, easily digestible texts in a variety of formats that had a clear, practical orientation—and that knowledge helped them decide which parts of elite intellectual culture they wanted to use. At the end of all that, what they came up with was a manuscript that included a variety of texts representing the higher-level, more interpretive side of intellectual culture (the commentary and small tract) and the more practical, skills-based forms of devotion that were more appropriate for ordinary laypeople. That, to me, tells us that the owner already had a pretty good sense of what sort of "beneficial activities" worked best for them, but they were also willing to push themselves a bit to learn even more about how the various liturgical and artistic devotional practices could help them follow the "inner life." Based on the fact that this book survived in such good condition and shows so many signs of physical use, I think we can say that this practical devotional collection functioned in exactly the way it was supposed to. In fact, it worked so well that the owner felt empowered to add a text of their very own, one that fit it perfectly with everything that made this devotional collection a success.

I can't say this for certain, of course, but I think professional medieval intellectuals would have been really happy with how the manuscript in Inc. 1699 turned out. In it, they would have seen the work of someone who, while not an expert themselves, had confidently and effectively taken elements from elite intellectual culture and creatively re-combined them into a book that helped them make progress towards salvation. In other words, the pros would have seen proof that everything they were trying to teach amateur audiences like Inc. 1699's owners was actually getting through to them. On that note—and this is really important—I want to emphasize that manuscripts like Inc. 1699 would not have been possible *without the full participation* of those elite, professional-level intellectuals. They knew that giving unadulterated specialist content in Latin to non-experts was not a recipe

---

29 De Boor, "Ein spät-mittelhochdeutsch Glossengedicht über das *Salve Regina*."

for success, so they had to do the difficult work of condensing, excerpting, editing, translating, and adapting that material so that uninitiated laypeople could work with it. For a good example of that, we need look no further than our old pal Henry Suso, who incorporated translated excerpts of the Thomas Aquinas's emphatically-elite *Summa theologiae* into his *Little Book of Wisdom*, one of the "good books" in *The Exemplar*.[30] In other words, having put in the effort to make this content accessible, those same elites handed it off to their non-expert audiences and let them make it into something that was their very own, just like the owner of Inc. 1699 did. In the end, both sides got what they wanted, which is the beauty of Audience Empowerment.

How to Let Go

For me, vernacular devotional manuscripts like Inc. 1699 are just the sort of billboard material that medievalists today need to see. It's a reminder of what is possible if we could, like our medieval predecessors, make Audience Empowerment a real priority for the field. This might sound like a scary thought. Because, when you get right down to it, Audience Empowerment is really about letting go (even a little bit) of your authority as an expert *and* the control you have over what happens to your work when it gets into the hands of non-experts. Especially in an age where some *extremely* non-expert groups have found ways to use medieval culture that support violent racist ideologies, it might seem like too much to ask to open the door to the field and let the non-experts in.

If that's the way you're feeling right now, I totally get that. Audience Empowerment requires a level of vulnerability that most academics simply don't feel comfortable with. But, if I may say so, I think a lot of that fear and doubt is really coming from Gatekeeping, which still keeps alive the elitist worries of the nineteenth century, fooling us into thinking that welcoming non-experts into the field is a sign of weakness or some sort of drag on the field. If you can step away from that, as I did when I got to the Newberry, I think you'll find the prospect of opening up the field to be not so scary after all. There's one particular experience of mine that stands out, and it started a few months into my postdoc in 2016, at a meeting to discuss launching an online portal for all the digital content related to the project. The Newberry's Communications department, directed at that time by my colleague Alex Teller, wanted to have at least some digital projects ready to go at the launch, in order to build interest for the exhibition to come. The Digital Ini-

30 Retucci, "Heinrich Seuse, Thomas Von Aquin und die 'Summa Theologiae Deutsch.'"

tiatives and Services Department (DIS) was also there, and they specifically requested something that included crowdsourced transcriptions, since their experience had taught them that audiences usually responded enthusiastically to those types of resources.

I wasn't immediately convinced by this idea; Gatekeeping still had a pretty good hold on me, so I doubted that non-experts would be able to do anything with the early modern manuscripts that featured in the project. Nevertheless, I somewhat begrudgingly suggested that we could build a transcription resource around three English manuscripts that would be in the upcoming gallery exhibition: an eighteenth-century commonplace book, a manuscript copy of Cotton Mather's *Cases Concerning Witchcraft*, and, most intriguing of all, an enigmatic book then catalogued as *The Book of Magical Charms*, an anonymous (at the time) seventeenth-century manuscript that contained a variety of spells, charms, incantations, and mystical religious material of one kind or another.[31] Together with DIS, I helped develop a website called *Transcribing Faith*, a transcription tool that would give users the chance to transcribe and comment on these early modern sources. Through all that, I still wasn't all that excited about the source, until I wrote the introduction for the main page. There, inspired by conversations with DIS, I used some language that my graduate student self would have been surprised to hear me say: "Help us unlock the mysteries of these texts." After the portal was up and running, I had turned my attention to other things, but Alex had noticed that *Transcribing Faith* was getting some buzz from a couple of websites (*Atlas Obscura* and Smithsonian.com). I took part in a couple interviews in the last weeks of my Mellon fellowship that were fun, but I still wasn't thinking all that much about our little transcription resource. It was cool that some people were interested, but I just didn't think that, when it was all said and done, anybody other than experts and students in early modern history would pay much attention to it. I was wrong.

Only a few days after my fellowship ended in June, I received a text from Alex that stopped me in my tracks: *Transcribing Faith* had utterly and completely blown up, going viral in a way that no Newberry digital resource ever had. Just as DIS had predicted, a flood of people, plenty of whom didn't have advanced degrees, had rushed to the site to do just what I had asked them to do in the introduction: help us out. Within a span of just a few weeks, thousands of people from around the world—including highly-trained scholars alongside music teachers, business professionals, undergraduate students,

---

31 Kepplinger, "Rational Magic."

doctors, philosophers, practicing Wiccans, and general magic enthusiasts—had transcribed and corrected everything on the website. But that wasn't all, these same audiences were discussing, joking about, and promoting the resource and their experience with it on Reddit, Facebook, and other social media platforms. Not only that, within the site itself we found people comparing notes about their experiences, mentioning other manuscripts they'd seen elsewhere, and bouncing ideas off one another. It was a whole community of mostly amateur palaeographers and early modern enthusiasts that sprang up right before our eyes.

But wait, there's more! This enthusiastic community, quite against my expectations, really *did* help us learn more about our collections. Their work helped bring the book to the attention of librarians at the Middle Temple Library in London, who were able to determine that the seventeenth-century intellectual and lawyer Robert Ashley was the author and copier of our manuscript.[32] More than this, the non-professional users were excitedly sharing information with one another in the comments on the transcription tool, creating communities of amateur palaeographers that understood that they were working together to help the Newberry understand its own collections, which, in the end, is exactly what happened. Thanks to their efforts, we even had digital, word-searchable transcriptions of three more Newberry manuscripts for future scholars and Newberry patrons. Make no mistake, *Transcribing Faith* was a bigger success than any of us could have imagined, and while there were a lot of reasons why, in the end, the biggest one was exactly what DIS had said at the first meeting: people were excited that a prominent academic(-ish) institution was actually asking for their help. And boy, did they deliver.

I think we can see the same spirit behind the creation of the manuscript in Inc. 1699 and the other late medieval vernacular devotional manuscripts like it. They were, just like *Transcribing Faith* more than five centuries later, visible proof of the excitement, the interest, and the willingness of people outside of the academic elite to learn about and responsibly and accurately contribute to intellectual culture. I find that to be a very comforting thing when I think about the possibilities Audience Empowerment could bring to our field, especially when you consider how popular the Middle Ages are outside of academia. I've seen with my own eyes how non-medievalists of all kinds suddenly feel excitement, curiosity, and wonder when they encounter medieval manuscripts at the Newberry; how they can ask good questions

---

32 Satterley, "Robert Ashley and the Authorship of Newberry MS 5017."

and make connections between the past and present in exhibition tours; and how they spend their time, money, and effort to visit medieval places, work with medieval objects, and share their knowledge of medieval culture after they take my classes. In other words, the interest outside of academia in doing the work of understanding and talking about the Middle Ages—which, by the way, is *exactly what a medievalist does*—is very real, and is standing right there at the gate. All we need to do is open it.

Chapter 5

THE PUBLIC ENGAGEMENT GAME PLAN

AFTER THAT QUICK flight through five centuries of public engagement in medieval Europe, it's time now to talk about maybe the most important thing of all: how to *implement* that model today. Unfortunately, we can't just copy everything Peter Damian, Hildegard of Bingen, Henry Suso, and the anonymous owner of Inc. 1699 did in the Middle Ages and paste it into our modern day. As with anything from the medieval past, the strategies they followed and the assumptions that lay behind them were plugged into a cultural context that no longer exists, and recreating that context as they knew it is not really an option for us. Fortunately, medievalists today do not need to become hermits, prophets, cart-drivers, or late medieval urban dwellers to adopt any of these medieval solutions. Instead, all we need to do is to focus on the public engagement tools themselves in order to isolate some basic but effective mindsets and practices that can be adapted into our context more easily. Having done that, it's time to focus on how you, dear reader, can incorporate all those medieval solutions into your own work.

That's why I like to think of this final chapter as a "game plan." By the time you've finished reading this, I'd like for you to have a good sense of how you might start laying the groundwork for doing effective public engagement based on whatever expertise or interest in medieval studies you either already have or are working to develop. Here's how we'll do it. First, I'll lay out all the cards by briefly going through the whole medieval public engagement model again. Then, I'll recommend some simple activities you can do to start practicing each of the four medieval solutions right now, at the same time as you're doing (or learning to do) everything else that a professional medievalist needs to do. Again, even though I'm talking mainly to medievalists here, I think these same activities can work for scholars in any other humanities field, as well. As you'll see, these suggested activities are neither super labour-intensive nor terribly time-consuming; their main purpose is to get you really thinking about how you can effectively engage audiences outside academia with your medieval expertise. The more you practice these methods and mindsets (especially if you're early in your career), the better prepared you'll be to build productive connections with all kinds of audiences when you're done.

At the end of this chapter, I hope you'll be able to see a way out of the public engagement funk medieval studies is in. After all, most of the ideas I have about putting the medieval model into practice are about changing one's mindset more than anything else; if you adopt these medieval solutions, you'll find yourself thinking quite differently about what you know about the Middle Ages and what impact it can have. Once you've gotten past the field's structural roadblocks, I'm confident you'll be able to ask the right kinds of questions and give the right kinds of answers in the right kinds of ways to help all kinds of audiences outside academia see the value in what you know about the Middle Ages. If you're a grad student, adjunct, or independent scholar worried about the job market, I think this chapter will help you learn how your work can help make you an appealing candidate to employers of all kinds. On the other end of the spectrum, if you're a more senior academic or tenured professor, I hope this chapter will help you advocate for the field in your department and/or institution, recruit more students, and support developing or early-career medievalists to develop effective public engagement skills as well. In short, I hope this model will help every medievalist set themselves, their colleagues, and the field up for success in the future.

Recapping the Medieval Model of Public Engagement

The medieval model begins with the Life of Service Conviction. As we saw with Peter Damian, this mentality makes it possible to do all the work necessary to make some kind of impact in the world. Thanks to the Life of Service Conviction, intellectuals felt a profound sense of responsibility to use their prodigious knowledge and highly-specialized skillsets to make some kind of meaningful difference in the world outside their elite circle. Even they knew that was a huge challenge, but because the Life of the Mind Excuse wasn't standing in their way, it was one that they confidently embraced. We can see that going on in all the work they produced, which was carefully shaped and packaged in ways that would get their expertise out in the world most successfully. In Damian's case, as we saw, this meant expressing himself mainly through letters, the genre that was public and persuasive enough to make people understand how they had to think and behave in the world.

That conviction, in turn, made it obvious that professional medieval intellectuals needed Genre Diversity to be successful. Blissfully free of Genre Dependency, they embraced the chance to be creative about how they shared their knowledge with everyone else. Hildegard of Bingen's career is a testament to this; she understood perfectly that the spiritual message the Living

Light commanded her to share was too big and too important to be contained in just one genre. If she was going to convince everyone to start embodying monastic virtues, she needed to broadcast that message in as many different genres as she possibly could, so that she could offer her diverse audience multiple points of access to the content of her visions. Importantly, though, the *Riesencodex* reminds us that, despite their differences, all those expressions were equally a part of the same mission, and, thus, equally valuable. Hildegard was exceptional in a lot of ways, but not in this; the diverse body of work left to us by medieval intellectuals show that they too understood the value of sharing their expertise in a variety of formats.

That realization made it easier for intellectuals to get out of their proverbial carts, roll up their proverbial robes, and wade into the proverbial mud to do some Audience Development. Elite intellectuals, despite all their lofty training, recognized the simple truth that it's easier to make a difference with an audience that you know very well, but getting to that point takes more than the wishful thinking and luck that the General Public Fallacy relies on. They knew that it took the kind of time, effort, and patience we saw in Henry Suso's decades-long service to Dominican nuns. In all that time, Suso never took anything for granted; he made sure that he nurtured the relationship he had with the sisters in all the ways that he could, especially by being present with them and listening to them. Ultimately, all his effort putting his audience first paid off in more ways than one; this mutually-beneficial relationship both made his own work better and helped bring it to audiences well beyond Dominican convents in the German lands, which ultimately allowed him to serve his neighbours as much as Eternal Wisdom wanted him to.

I can imagine that the last part of the medieval model of public engagement, Audience Empowerment, was the most difficult one for professional intellectuals to do in medieval Europe. Then, as now, there was a lot of safety and comfort in Gatekeeping, and there were plenty of intellectuals in medieval Europe who wanted to keep certain aspects of their work out of the hands of the uninitiated. But, despite all those concerns, there were still many elite intellectuals who were willing to open the door to intellectual culture so non-experts, even ordinary laypeople, could come in. The manuscript we see in Inc. 1699, for all the things we don't know about its owner, is clear proof of that. On the one hand, we can see all the hard work of translating, excerpting, and adapting that professionals must have done to make all the theological and devotional material in the book accessible to laypeople. But we can also see an ordinary layperson confidently and enthusiastically devote their financial and intellectual resources to creating, using, and even adding to a personalized devotional program for themselves and, quite possibly, others as well. I think professionals would have been delighted at that, because, in the end, books like Inc. 1699 were physical evidence that all their public engagement was working.

I've found a lot of comfort and inspiration in this medieval model. Precisely because we have so much evidence that these solutions worked in the medieval past, I'm confident that an adapted version of that model can also work for us today. And, as I mentioned earlier, I don't think it requires us to also get degrees in marketing or communications at the same time as our advanced medieval studies degree to do it. All we really need to do is avoid the structural roadblocks that are holding us back from seeing what kind of impact our expertise can make. So, in the sections that follow, you'll find some simple activities that you can do to make public engagement a central part of the work you are already doing as a medievalist.

How to Implement the Life of Service Conviction: Make an Echoes List

Let's start where the medieval intellectuals started, because, not to sound like a broken record or anything, the whole public engagement endeavour really begins with the Life of Service Conviction. As we saw in chapter 1, medieval studies' future depends on all of us, even those who are just in it to contribute to scholarship or out of love for the weird coolness of the Middle Ages (both of which are perfectly wonderful things, by the way), being able to confidently and compellingly talk about the value the field creates for everyone else. This medieval solution can help us do that. The end goal here is a field that *insists*—repeatedly, publicly, and sometimes even forcefully—that medieval studies are relevant to our contemporary society, and that there is room in the field for everyone.

That kind of advocacy doesn't come naturally to everyone, and it certainly isn't taught in a traditional graduate program. Medievalists have gotten better at doing this in the recent past, but there's still a long way to go. So I'd like to suggest an activity that, over time, will help you learn how to start building up your awareness of the ways in which medieval studies can intervene in areas outside academia, whether you are starting a graduate program or entering emeritus status. Before you even start it, though, you might need to make a slight but significant adjustment to how you think about what you, as a medievalist, actually *know*. Remember, the Life of the Mind Excuse would have you believe that all you know is some very specific information about a narrowly-defined aspect of something in the distant past that matters only to a niche group of scholars. If you want to get more in line with the Life of Service Conviction, though, what you *know* is this: how and why human beings think and act in all kinds of ways. See the difference? Think about it for a second; medievalists have expert-level knowledge of how and why human beings in the Middle Ages did things like solve problems, manage money and resources, deal with emotions, interact with their environment, start and resolve conflicts, make art, and all kinds of other things. Well guess what? Humans are, right this minute, *still doing all of those things*. Sure, they don't do them in the same ways or for the same reasons as medieval people, but the fact remains that all the work you will put in (or have put in) to become a medievalist means that you will have a lot to say and contribute to any attempt to understand, guide, or influence how people think about and do things today. In short, this little shift in perspective can help you start realizing that your "niche" expertise *matters right now*.

Once you've got that idea firmly in your head, you're ready for the activity: making an "Echoes List." It concerns what I call "echoes," which is a slightly fancy term for those moments when something medieval reminds you of something modern, or vice versa. So, for example, if learning about Louis IX resettling Levantine converts in France in the thirteenth century makes you think of immigration in Europe today, that's an echo. I've found that these echoes come at different volumes; some are pretty faint and weak ("This kind of makes me think of"), but others are loud and strong ("Oh man, this is *just like*"). I'm willing to bet that you hear these echoes quite a lot as you're going about your medievalist life, and that's where this activity comes in. You see, the Life of the Mind Excuse would have you ignore or downplay those echoes, but the Life of Service Conviction wants you to take them *very* seriously. That's because they are signs, however slight, that the things we know about the medieval past can actually contribute something to modern concerns. So, the point of this activity is to help you start using those echoes to explain what your work can do for the so-called "real world."

Here's how it works. The first thing to do is simply to *pay attention* to the echoes when they show up. When they happen, I encourage you to take a moment to think about why it came up for you. Why do you think [medieval thing] reminded you of [modern thing], or vice versa? How strong would you say this echo is? Once you get a bit better at paying attention to echoes, it's time to take some notes, something I assume you're already doing all the time. So, at first, when you hear an echo, make a note. These notes don't need to be long or discursive if you don't want them to be. At this point, the goal is to start making a habit out of recognizing and articulating the connections between the Middle Ages and the modern day.

If you're a graduate student, this habit will come in very handy when you enter the more advanced stages of your graduate work, that is, the time when you become an expert in some aspect of medieval culture. As your engagement with medieval stuff intensifies, I expect the echoes you encounter will start getting louder, stronger, and, quite likely, more focused. I think the same process will also happen if you're a more advanced medievalist, especially when you're starting a new project. Either way, when the echoes intensify, you'll be ready for the next stage of the activity: compiling a list of echoes in a notebook, spreadsheet, bulletin board, whatever. The entries don't need to be super long or detailed; something like "Bernard of Clairvaux flipping out over losing his seal makes me think about fake social media accounts" will do just fine. The important thing is to record whatever connection you're seeing between the medieval and the modern. Every now and again, you should read over that list and think about what it's telling you about the broader implications of your work. Your results may vary; you may find that your project is resonating with all kinds of things in the modern day, or (more likely, in my experience) you'll see a relatively short list of very strong resonances with a few modern things. If you have the chance, it would also be a good idea to set aside some time to try and learn why these resonances are happening for you. If something especially intriguing comes up, add that to the list, too.

The upshot of this activity is that, by the time you complete your PhD or your project, you'll also have a list of the possible ways your particular medieval expertise connects to modern concerns, practices, and institutions. This, in turn, will help you understand—and help *others* understand—what you can do with your medieval expertise. Had I done this activity while I was working on my dissertation, for example, I would have realized much sooner that my expert knowledge of medieval letter-writing could be useful for political campaigns, public relations firms, or marketing departments, because I understood how individuals and institutions could safely and responsibly communicate their ideas and brands in a relatively unregulated media climate. You will learn different things from your Echoes List, I imagine, but the overall result will be the same: you'll know how your specialized medieval expertise can serve a variety of modern publics.

Implementing Genre Diversity: Medieval Resource Reviews

I think implementing Genre Diversity should be easier for you than the other solutions, since we already have so many good examples of medievalists sharing their expertise in innovative ways that you could use for inspiration. But, even with those examples, medieval studies' debilitating case of Genre Dependency still makes it too difficult for many medievalists to imagine how producing anything other than a scholarly publication will advance their career, especially while they're still in graduate school. So, in this section, I'm going to introduce you to activity that will, I hope, help you start to think about how you can share your expertise in different genres.

Success with this activity really boils down to answering two simple questions that I first heard in 2016 in the chilly, windowless office of my friend and colleague Jennifer Wolfe, who was then the Digital Librarian in the Newberry's Digital Initiatives and Services department. I had gone there discuss what kinds of digital resources we might put together for the Religious Change project, and I was nervous. You see, during my interview for the job, the one question I think I could have answered better (that's a polite way of saying "totally bombed") was about digital humanities. I didn't have a lot of experience with them at all, and I was quite worried about having to suddenly take the lead in developing them. So at the beginning of our meeting, I launched into a long (as I remember it) rant about everything I didn't know about digital humanities. After patiently sitting through all of that, Jen simply asked "Well, what do you want people to know?" After thinking for a bit, I answered that I had never quite been able to get my students to understand just how important the technology of the pamphlet was to Martin Luther's success. I had tried everything: I talked about it a lot in class, I assigned scholarly readings making that point, and I showed a bunch of images of pamphlets in my lecture PowerPoints, but my students just never seemed to "get it" in the way that I wanted.

After that, Jen asked me another question, one that I realize now is the whole key to Genre Diversity: "*How can you help them learn that*?" In all my time as a professional medievalist, I had never seriously thought about a question like that before; as far as I knew, I had already done everything I possibly could. When Jen asked it, though, it dawned on me that there were other genres that could express an important historical fact that the traditional scholarly publication, lecture, or PowerPoint couldn't. Our conversation led us to develop an interactive map, *Tracking the Luther Controversy*, that showed how the Reformation took place through pamphlets.[1] Finally, I had a way for students to visualize debates over Luther's ideas pinging from one pamphlet to another, which helped the students see how much work pamphlets were doing and how much more Luther used them than his Catholic opponents, which helped him survive the church's attempts to silence him. Much to our delight, we later learned that the resource, as one instructor put it on social media, "gave great context" when other instructors taught their students about the Reformation.

These two questions—"what do you want people to know?" and "how can you help them know it?"—are, I now realize, the cornerstone of developing Genre Diversity. The second question is particularly critical, because it's the one most concerned with format and genre. To go back to my pamphlet example, this was the question that made me think about *how* I could express the urgent, rapid-fire nature of pamphlet literature in the sixteenth century, something that didn't come across in the more traditional scholarly formats I'd tried. To help you learn that as well, I'd like to suggest an activity that will hopefully help you develop an understanding of the variety of ways in which different formats can express your knowledge.

Since medieval intellectuals were much better at public engagement than we are right now, the sources they left to us (which, again, happen to be the entire foundation of this field) were carefully designed to effectively engage different audiences in a variety of ways. Collectively, then, the sources we look at in our research (chronicles, poetry, music, visual art, architecture, etc.) are like a set of tools that can be used to share content with various audiences. So, the better you are at understanding how those sources functioned as tools of public engagement in their own time, the better you'll be at understanding what contemporary public engagement formats you could use to tell people about them now. The key to developing that mindset is an activity that I always assign to students in my graduate seminar on digital humanities that I've taught a few times at the Newberry: writing reviews. Now, to be clear, I'm not talking about the formal one thousand-word scholarly reviews you'll find in journals or on listservs, but the kind of reviews that ultimately explain whether you should patronize a business, buy or use a particular product, visit a museum on vacation, and the like.

There are two levels to this activity, as I understand it. You could do them in whatever order you want, although I think the first level works better in the early stages of a research project, course design, or graduate program, when you'll probably be exposed to a wider range of medieval sources

1 https://publications.newberry.org/digital/luther-map/.

thanks to your various preparations. Here's how it works. Whenever you engage with a medieval source of some kind, you should take some time (just a few minutes is all you need) to ask yourself a set of questions about it. As before, you could write your answers to those questions down if you want, or just do it in your head. Either works. The questions you ask here are geared towards understanding your gut reaction to the source, that is, why you liked, disliked, or felt indifferent about it. You can make up your own questions, but here's a few just to get you started: Do I like/dislike/feel indifferent about this source? Why do I feel that way? How do I wish this source were different? How does this compare to other sources that I like/dislike/feel indifferent about? After asking yourself these questions, you should answer them, *but*...this is important...don't do any research. Don't go learning all about literary theory or try to make yourself into an expert before you say anything, just go with what you feel and what you observe. As best you can, try to make sure that your answers have some detail. For example, say things like "I didn't like the *Summa Theologiae* because I'm a visual learner and there was too much text" instead of "I didn't like the *Summa Theologiae* because it's boring."

Again, you don't have to write any of this down if you don't want to; the point is that you start to make connections between your reactions to a particular medieval source and the rhetorical and technical ways in which that source works. After all, as we learned in chapter 2, medieval intellectuals were a lot more creative than we are, so the expressions of their expertise often engage audiences in ways (visually, aurally, textually, materially) that our scholarly publications don't. In this first level of the review activity, you're basically learning how to recognize the many ways in which medieval sources *talk to you*. Like any form of media, some of those ways will work for you, and some of them won't, but either way it doesn't matter. As long as you're thinking about how a medieval source speaks to a particular audience (i.e., you), you're well on your way to Genre Diversity.

The next level of this activity comes at a later stage in your project's development (if you're a graduate student, this would be after you've started researching for a dissertation or thesis). At that stage, you'll have chosen a particular medieval source (or group of sources) that you'll get to know *extremely* well, and you'll need that background here. At this level, your goal should be to periodically stop and make a review of your source that *recommends* it to a different audience. To do that, you should use another set of questions that try to dig further into how your medieval sources work. Again, you can make up your own questions, but here are some suggestions: How does this source express its content? What would someone need to know or do to use this source properly? What sort of audience would find this approach useful? That last question is probably the most important one; whatever you're working with, you should try to think of some general type of audience that would respond well to how your source works. Something like this: "If you like colourful and shiny things, you would love to look at this illuminated Book of Hours!"

The whole point of the review activity is to help you recognize how different genres and formats engage their audiences. That's not something we can really get from scholarly publications, because that genre offers only one kind of engagement: the scholarly way. That's why the activity focuses on medieval sources; as we saw in chapter 2, they were produced in an intellectual culture that was much more naturally creative than ours, so they usually share their content in multiple ways that could appeal to various audiences at once. This activity will, I hope, help you become more familiar with that concept, which will then help you understand how those sources can speak to modern audiences today. It will also remind you how fun and interesting the source is, which will make it easier for you to get other people excited about it. Once you do that, I think you'll find it easier to imagine how you can tell those audiences something about medieval culture that a scholarly publication won't allow, and appreciate how this variety of expression gives a more complete and accurate picture of medieval culture.

How to Implement Audience Development: Get Involved

Like I said in chapter 3, Audience Development is a medieval solution that doesn't require a lot of adaptation. Every one of the stages we can draw out of Henry Suso's engagement with the Dominican sisters is something that would, generally speaking, be just as effective today as it was in the fourteenth century. So, if you want to develop an audience for your medieval work outside of academia, all you have to do is 1) commit yourself to doing it; 2) identify a specific audience to connect with; 3) be present with that audience to build a relationship with it; 4) listen to what the members of that audience want, need, or are interested in; and 5) share your knowledge in a way that matches those interests, wants, and needs. Easy, right? Well, not really. Audience Development still requires a lot of time and work, which means it is probably the most difficult medieval public engagement approach to work into your professional development or day-to-day work.

But fear not! I assure you there are some ways you can lay a foundation for successful Audience Development wherever you are in your career. Step 1, for example, is a freebie; you can commit yourself to developing an audience long before you actually have the chance to do it, so you're already 20 per cent of the way there! Seriously, though, I think the activity that will set you up for the most success with Audience Development comes down to two words: get involved. Actually, sorry, let me add a couple more words to that: get involved *in something outside academia*. If you're a grad student; I bet you've heard that before; it has (thankfully) become pretty common for graduate programs to encourage students to "do something else" from time to time to help preserve their physical, spiritual, and mental well-being. You also might have heard from former academics giving career advice that "diversifying" your time is a great way to develop skills and contacts that will make you an appealing candidate for jobs outside academia.[2] If you're not a graduate student, I expect that you've already been diversifying your time, but if you haven't, I think it would be a good idea for you to start.

In any case, however it is that you get involved, you will also get better at developing audiences for your medieval expertise along the way. Whatever your "something else" is will give you the opportunity to get to know a specific audience better by spending time with them, sharing a particular experience with them, listening to them, and learning from them. With that in your back pocket, the only step that's left is figuring out how to share your content with them in way that you know they'll respond to (see previous activity). Once you do, quite suddenly, you'll find yourself 80 per cent of the way to mastering Audience Development.

How you "get involved" is pretty simple: find an organization, class, activity, or group of some kind that fits with your interests, passions, wants, or needs and, well, get involved in it. This could mean volunteering at a nonprofit devoted to a cause that you care deeply about, joining a recreational league for a sport that you enjoy playing, getting involved at your child's school, working as a staffer on a political campaign you support, taking some kind of active role in your religious community, or attending a class to learn a new skill you've always wanted to try (like playing a musical instrument or making pottery). If getting involved in public isn't your thing, that's okay, too; you can learn just as much about what people outside academia want and need even if you just sit quietly in the back of a room, watch from the sidelines, or log into to an online community. Oh, and don't forget that spending time with your friends and loved ones 100 per cent counts as "getting involved," too. For our purposes here, the goal is to find yourself—in whatever way you're most comfortable—among a bunch of non-medi-

2 Cao, "Freeing the PhD."

evalists who also happen to share a particular interest with you. That really matters, because when people share a common interest, it's easier for them to talk to each other. And when people talk to each other, they learn a lot about each other.

Ideally, once you've been involved in your "something" for a while, you'll feel more comfortable sharing your medieval interests with this non-expert group. If you get to that point, just remember that you don't need to act like an expert in those non-academic spaces; nobody there is trying to test you or judge your worthiness as a medievalist. Hopefully, they'll just be interested in hearing more about another interest you have. But whether or not you talk about the nuts and bolts of your dissertation, class, or book project, I want you to think about getting involved as another way to make you a better medievalist. In fact, I wouldn't be at all surprised if diversifying your time helps you understand your work even better, because you'll have a clearer sense of how you might share it outside a scholarly field.

That happened for me during the last couple years of graduate school, when I joined the Adult Spiritual Growth Team at St. Paul's Lutheran Church in my hometown of Waukegan, Illinois. Working with the pastors to develop one-off devotional meetings and curricula for the Lenten spiritual education series started out as "something else" that I could do outside of my work to keep me sane, but I soon found it gave me a really interesting perspective on the kinds of spiritual instruction medieval religious thinkers were trying to do in their letters. Talking about that sort of thing with my pastors, who obviously had a lot to say about it, helped me get my head around how people like Hildegard and Peter Damian and all the rest condensed things like discussions of the Trinity into a form that ordinary folks could grasp. And that, as we saw in chapter 1, is something that later helped me engage other audiences in medieval history. So yes, diversify your time, but when you do, keep an open mind for how your "something else" can be an opportunity for you to plant seeds now that will grow into enthusiastic and interested audiences for medieval studies later.

Implementing Audience Empowerment: The Grocery Store Scenario

And now for the final boss. Even if you're a seasoned medievalist, it might be a while before you feel ready to tackle Audience Empowerment, and I wouldn't blame you. In some ways, this becomes harder to do the more expertise you gain, because you're much more aware of everything that non-experts *don't* know about your medieval topic. For graduate students, it might be even more difficult. After all, don't you have to wait until you have some recognized authority in the subject before you can, as I put it earlier, let it go? To a certain extent, that's true, I suppose. But remember, at its core, Audience Empowerment is as simple as making people who aren't professional medievalists feel welcomed and valued within the field. And that is something you can start doing at any time in your career by being comfortable talking about being a medievalist in any setting, before any group, at any time.

Like we talked about in chapter 4, it's surprisingly rare—even in this age of increased attention to advocacy—for medievalists to be able to do this outside of academic or academic-adjacent spaces. We have Gatekeeping to thank for that, since it makes us think that medievalists are welcomed and valued *only* in those spaces, which can make us feel hesitant, nervous, or downright worried about what people would do or say if we tried to be medievalists anywhere else. I don't have any numbers to back this up or anything, but I think non-medievalists can sense the weird vibes we give off when we're outside academia, which only makes it less likely that non-academics will feel welcome in the field. That's why it's important to give off a different vibe when we're out in the "real world," one that is much more receptive to non-experts who think that the Middle Ages are cool and interesting. Spoiler alert, the traditional form of graduate training will not teach you how to do this, so I'd like to suggest an activity that, I think, can.

That would be the Grocery Store Scenario, a hypothetical exercise for you to practice talking to non-academics about being a medievalist in non-academic spaces. This exercise is based on a hypothetical question that a terrific former student of mine, Caitlin Branum Thrash, asked me at a conference. As you go through your professional life, I think you should make time—it really shouldn't take more than five minutes—to run through this scenario a few times, say, every time you advance to another stage of your program (coursework, orals, proposal, research year, job market, etc.) or start another project. You could do it completely in your own head, or you could say it out loud or write it out. If you're feeling especially motivated, you and some other medievalists (or non-medievalists!) could act it out. Regardless, the important thing is that you take it as seriously as you can.

Here's the scenario. Imagine yourself in standing in the checkout line at the grocery store. Someone a few carts ahead is taking longer at the register, and you share a knowing glance with the person ahead of you. That person, who is clearly not an academic, then strikes up a conversation with you. After a few pleasantries (that person up there is taking *forever*), they ask you what you do for a living. Without hesitation, you answer that you're a medievalist, and that you study [insert your main interest(s) here]. In response, the stranger replies, "Wow! That's cool!" Now comes the most important part: *what do you do next?*

There are a whole range of possible things you could do at this point, of course, and I won't try to list them all here, but I think they would all fall into one of two categories: unproductive and productive. The former category includes all the answers that Gatekeeping wants us to give, such as "quickly change the subject," "just say I'm a student/teacher because they won't get it anyway," or "use a bunch of jargon." The latter category, on the other hand, is what Audience Empowerment wants you to give, such as "I agree, it *is* cool!" or "Oh yeah, I love it, how about you?" or "Totally. What do you think is cool about it?" See the difference? The unproductive responses ultimately maintain a distance between medievalists and non-medievalists, the productive ones shorten or even eliminate that distance.

The productive responses do that by, as it were, handing the baton *back* to the non-expert and giving them the chance to speak. This really isn't as radical as Gatekeeping makes it seem. When it comes down to it, we should want to talk about the Middle Ages with people who think they're cool and interesting, *because we also think they're cool and interesting*. It's right here, in conversations just like this, that we can build that long-sought-for bridge between all of the popular interest in medieval stuff with the work we do as medievalists. The Grocery Store Scenario is a way for you to prepare for those critical conversations by imagining how you can talk about your work in a way that makes non-experts feel welcomed and valued.

This is not something one normally does in graduate school or during the usual course of an academic year, but it is something I do all the time at the Newberry in collection presentations, exhibition tours, and random encounters in the reading room. In all those cases, I do my best to *not* sound like a scholar; instead, I try to come across as someone who's excited about and interested in medieval things. I have a couple strategies for doing that, too, and I'm happy to share those with you.

STRATEGY 1: *Don't say "actually."* "Actually" was one of my staple vocabulary words when I was teaching in grad school and as an adjunct; I used it a lot whenever students made an observation or declaration about the Middle Ages that, in my view, wasn't quite right. So, for example, if a student said, "The church wanted the stuff in this book to be a secret because it's written in Latin," I would respond with "Actually, plenty of laypeople could read Latin in the Middle Ages." I don't recall it ever having much of a reaction in the classroom, but at the Newberry, I noticed that people's enthusiasm or excitement noticeably dropped every time I said it. The reason why, I think, is that, generally speaking, people don't like to be told that they're wrong, which is exactly what I was doing. Though no one ever said so out loud, their reactions told me that "actually" was a sign of me invoking my expert authority to shut a non-expert down. So, instead of doing that, I try to answer those comments in a way that validates their initial interpretation, like this: "Ah, that is a good observation! It's true that most people in medieval Europe didn't know Latin, so a lot people couldn't read this book. But you know what's interesting? There were a lot of books made for laypeople that were in Latin, so that suggests that at least some of them could read it. So maybe this book wasn't so secret after all." That second answer was longer, to be sure, but I've found that people usually don't mind, so long as I don't seem to shut them down by saying "actually."

STRATEGY 2: *Admit Ignorance*. As you probably know, it's hard to feel comfortable doing this in academia, where it seems that admitting you don't know something is a sign of weakness, even if you're a tenured professor (Quick sidebar: it is not). I thought that mindset didn't make any sense while I was in grad school, and yet I still found myself staying silent at lectures or in discussions when I didn't feel I was an expert more times than I like to admit. At the Newberry, though, it's a different story. If I'm not an expert in something, I'll say so ("Well, I'm not an expert in that"). If I get asked a question I don't know the answer to, I'll say that too ("Good question! I'd have to look that up"). And, if I'm not sure whether my answer is right, I'll also say that ("I think it could be [answer], but I could be wrong..."). This strategy is *extremely* helpful for making the field more welcoming, because it helps get rid of the common perception that you have to know *everything* about the Middle Ages before you can say *anything* about it. The people who aren't experts are, for the most part, already perfectly aware that they don't know everything about medieval culture, and it seems that they find it comforting when "experts" like me admit that we don't either.

STRATEGY 3: *Share the mic*. I've noticed that, when we medievalists get the opportunity to talk about a medieval thing in a non-academic space, it's hard for us to resist jumping up on the stage, grabbing the mic and talking about it like we're giving a lecture or a conference plenary. That means monologuing about something for a long time and sharing a ton of details without giving the other person a chance to speak. But I've learned at the Newberry that, while people love to learn new things, they usually don't love being lectured to. As Henry Suso knew, conversations are a whole lot better for building productive connections with other people, so I try to do everything I can to teach people about medieval things that way. When I do—and I can't emphasize this enough—there are four words I always say that matter more than almost any other, and that I encourage you to use as much as you can.

Ready? Here they are: *what do you think*? These words are the whole key to Audience Empowerment. I expect they're already very familiar to you, especially if you've been teaching; medievalists ask their non-specialist students this question all the time, which makes it all the more strange to me that we don't seem to ask it in any other context. People excited about the Middle Ages (and, again, there are more of those than you might think) *want* to talk about it with experts, but we rarely give them the chance to do it. So, whenever I say, "What do you think?" to someone at the Newberry, I'm really giving them an invitation to join me in the work that professional medievalists do: try to understand why medieval people did what they did. By sharing the mic, I help people feel not only like they're allowed to do that work too, but that I'd be happy if they did.

I don't expect you to have a ton of success with the Grocery Store Scenario right away. Depending on how long you've been in your program or teaching at a university, it could be hard to imagine talking about what you do in an open and inviting way. If that's the case for you, keep at it! Like any medieval intellectual knew, the more you run through those hypothetical scenarios, the easier it will be for you to make a non-medievalist feel like there is a place for them in our cool and interesting field. Oh, and one more thing: there will always be times when we as medievalists need to pull rank and tell people they're wrong, like anytime we see someone promoting the white supremacist version of the medieval past. In those cases, it's our responsibility to make sure we set the record straight (you can definitely use "actually" in this case). But the rest of the time, we should be going about our work outside of academia in a spirit of humility instead of authority. That, really, is what Audience Empowerment is all about: letting others use their perspectives, knowledge, and enthusiasm to make our field better.

And there you have it! Successful public engagement in four stages. If you work on incorporating these activities into your graduate training or your ongoing professional development, I'm convinced that they'll help you develop the skills and mindsets you need to build productive connections with various audiences outside academia about medieval studies. Right now, it may seem difficult to imagine that making a list of echoes, writing reviews no one will see, getting involved in something unrelated to your work, or pretending to be stuck in line at a grocery store will do anything to solve the crisis of medieval studies. But the more you work on them, the better at public engagement you'll become, because you'll have exactly what your medieval predecessors had (and what Sad Ovid doesn't): the confidence that your work matters to the world *and* the skills you need to effectively explain why. Good luck!

BIBLIOGRAPHY

Manuscripts and Archival Materials

Chicago, The Newberry Library

Apocalypsis Sancti Johannis. Germany, ca. 1470. VAULT folio Inc. 15.

Naso, Publius Ovidius. *Tutti gli libri de Ouidio Metamorphoseos*. Venice: Niccolò Zuppino, 1522. Case Y 672 .09647.

Thomas of Kempen. *Ein ware nachuolgung Cristi*. Augsburg: Anton Sorg, 1486. Inc. 1699.

Wiesbaden, Hochschul- und Landesbibliothek RheinMain

Hildegard of Bingen. *Riesencodex*. Rupertsberg, ca. 1180/1190?. Hs. 2.

Wolfenbüttel, Herzog August Bibliothek

Hildegard of Bingen et al. *Liber trium virorum et trium spiritualium virginum*. Paris: Stephanus Briensis, 1513. A: 456.11 Theol. 2° (1).

Suso, Henry. *Heinrich Susos Buch genannt der Süse*. Nürnberg(?), ca. 1473. Cod. Guelf. 78.5 Aug. 2°.

Printed Primary Sources

Anselm of Bec. *The Prayers and Meditations of St. Anselm with the Proslogion*. Translated by Sister Benedicta Ward. New York: Penguin, 2006.

Augustine of Hippo. *On Christian Teaching*. Translated by R. P. H. Green. Oxford: Oxford University Press, 2008.

Benedict of Nursia. *RB 1980: The Rule of St. Benedict in Latin and English with Notes*. Edited and translated by Timothy Fry et al. Collegeville: Liturgical, 1980. http://www.archive.osb.org/rb/text/toc.html, accessed October 15, 2024.

Cicero, Marcus Tullius. *De inventione*. Edited by Maria Greco. Galatina: Congedo, 1998.

Henry Suso. *Heinrich Seuse: Deutsche Schriften*. Edited by Karl Bihlmeyer. Stuttgart: Kohlhammer, 1907, repr. Frankfurt am Main: Minerva, 1961.

——. *Henry Suso, The Exemplar, with Two German Sermons*. Edited and translated by Frank Tobin. The Classics of Western Spirituality. New York: Paulist, 1989.

Hildegard of Bingen. *Epistolarium Hildegardis Bingensis*. Edited by Lieven Van Acker and Monkia Klaes. 3 vols. Corpus Christianorum Continuatio Medievalis 91–91B. Turnhout: Brepols, 1991–2001.

——. *The Letters of Hildegard of Bingen*. Translated by Joseph L. Baird and Radd K. Ehrman. 3 vols. Oxford: Oxford University Press, 1994–2004.

——. *Ordo virtutum*. Edited and translated by Audrey Ekdahl Davidson. Kalamazoo: Medieval Institute Publications, 1985.

——. *Ordo virtutum*. Edited by Peter Dronke. *Hildegardis Bingensis opera minora*, 479–521. Corpus Christianorum Continuatio Medievalis 226. Turnhout: Brepols, 2007.

——. *Scivias*. Edited by Adelgundis Führkötter. 2 vols. Corpus Christianorum Continuatio Medievalis 43–43A. Turnhout: Brepols, 1978.

——. *Scivias*. Translated by Mother Columba Hart and Jane Bishop. New York: Paulist, 1990.

Peter Damian. *Die Briefe des Petrus Damiani*. Edited by Kurt Reindel. 4 vols. Monumenta Germaniae Historica Briefe der deutschen Kaiserzeit 4. München: Harrassowitz, 1983–1993.

——. *The Letters of Peter Damian*. Translated by Owen Blum and Irven Resnick. 6 vols. Washington, DC: Catholic University of America Press, 1989–2005.

Pseudo-Cicero. *Rhetorica ad Herennium*. Edited by Friedhelm L. Müller. Aachen: Shaker, 1994.

Thomas of Kempen. *The Imitation of Christ*. Translated by Leo Sherley-Price. New York: Penguin, 1952.

Secondary Works

Albin, Andrew et al, eds. *Whose Middle Ages?: Teachable Moments for an Ill-used Past*. New York: Fordham University Press, 2019.

Altstatt, Alison. "The *Ordo virtutum* and Benedictine Monasticism." In *The Cambridge Companion to Hildegard of Bingen*. Edited by Jennifer Bain, 235–56. Cambridge: Cambridge University Press, 2021.

Anderson, Wendy Love. "The Context and Reception of Hildegard of Bingen's Visions." In *The Cambridge Companion to Hildegard of Bingen*. Edited by Jennifer Bain, 189–205. Cambridge: Cambridge University Press, 2021.

Bain, Jennifer, ed. *The Cambridge Companion to Hildegard of Bingen*. Cambridge: Cambridge University Press, 2021.

Bennett, Susan, ed. *Theatre Audiences: A Theory of Production and Reception*. New York: Routledge, 1990.

Bernhardt, Susanne. *Figur im Vollzug: Narrative Strukturen im religiösen Selbstentwurf der Vita Heinrich Seuses*. Tübingen: Narr Francke Attempto, 2016.

Biddick, Kathleen. *The Shock of Medievalism*. Durham: Duke University Press, 1998.

Blum, Owen J. *St. Peter Damian: His Teaching on the Spiritual Life*. Washington, DC: Catholic University of America Press, 1947.

Blumrich, Rüdiger. "Die Überlieferung der deutschen Schriften Heinrich Seuses: Ein Forschungsbericht." In *Heinrich Seuses Philosophia spiritualis: Quellen, Konzept, Formen, und Rezeption. Tagung Eichstätt 2.–4. Oktober 1994*. Edited by Rüdiger Blumrich and Philipp Kaiser, 189–201. Wiesbaden: Reichert, 1994.

Boivin, Katherine Morris. *Riemenschneider in Rothenburg: Sacred Space and Civic Identity in the Late Medieval City*. University Park: Pennsylvania State University Press, 2021.

Boyle, Rachel. "Envisioning New Economic Models for Public History, Part II: The Cultural Co-Op." *Omnia History Blog*, June 4, 2018. https://omniahistory.com/2018/06/envisioning-new-economic-models-for-public-history-part-ii-the-cultural-co-op/#more-359, accessed September 29, 2024.

Caccipuoti, Christine and Elizabeth Keohane-Burbidge, eds. *Independent Scholars Meet the World: Expanding Academia Beyond the Academy*. Lawrence: University Press of Kansas, 2020.

——. "Introduction: Finding and Defining the Independent Scholar." In *Independent Scholars Meet the World: Expanding Academia Beyond the Academy*. Edited by Christine Caccipuoti and Elizabeth Keohane-Burbidge, 1–25. Lawrence: University Press of Kansas, 2020.

Cao, Vay. "Freeing the PhD: Solving an Identity Crisis." In *Independent Scholars Meet the World: Expanding Academia Beyond the Academy*. Edited by Christine Caccipuoti and Elizabeth Keohane-Burbidge, 205–27. Lawrence: University Press of Kansas, 2020.

Carruthers, Mary. *The Craft of Thought: Meditation, Rhetoric, and the Making of Images, 400–1200*. New York: Cambridge University Press, 1998.

——, ed. *Rhetoric Beyond Words: Delight and Persuasion in the Arts of the Middle Ages*. Cambridge: Cambridge University Press, 2010.

Cassuto, Leonard. *The Graduate School Mess: What Caused It and How We Can Fix It*. Cambridge: Harvard University Press, 2015.

Constable, Giles. *The Reformation of the Twelfth Century*. New York: Cambridge University Press, 1996.

D'Arcens, Louise, ed. *The Cambridge Companion to Medievalism*. Cambridge: Cambridge University Press, 2016.

de Boor, H. "Ein spat-mittelhochdeutsch Glossengedicht über das *Salve Regina*." In *Märchen, Mythos, Dichtung: Festschrift zum 90. Geburtstag Friedrich von der Leyens*. Edited by Hugo Kuhn, 335–42. München: Beck, 1963.

Dinshaw, Carolyn. *How Soon is Now? Medieval Texts, Amateur Readers, and the Queerness of Time*. Durham: Duke University Press, 2012.

Dronke, Peter. "Hildegard of Bingen." In *Women Writers in the Middle Ages: A Critical Study of Texts from Perpetua (d. 203) to Marguerite Porete (d. 1310)*, 144–201. Cambridge: Cambridge University Press, 1984.

Eagleton, Terry. "Phenomenology, Hermeneutics, and Reception Theory." In *Literary Theory: An Introduction*, 47–78. 2nd ed. Malden: Blackwell, 2008.

Eisenberg, Merle with Cate Kurtz. "Executive Summary of Medieval Studies Academic-Positions Update." *The Medieval Academy of America Blog*. https://www.themedievalacademyblog.org/wp-content/uploads/2023/05/Medieval-Jobs-Summary-Report.pdf, accessed October 4, 2024.

Enders, Jody. "Visions with Voices: The Rhetoric of Memory and Music in Liturgical Drama." *Comparative Drama* 24, no. 1 (Spring 1990): 34–54.

Enders, Markus. *Gelassenheit und Abgeschiedenheit: Studien zur Deutschen Mystik*. Hamburg: Kovač, 2008.

Fassler, Margot. "Allegorical Architecture in *Scivias*: Hildegard's Setting for the *Ordo virtutum*." *Journal of the American Musicological Society* 67, no. 2 (Summer 2014): 317–78.

Feenstra, Sanne et al. "Contextualizing the Impostor 'Syndrome.'" *Frontiers in Psychology* 11 (2020). Posted November 12, 2020. https://doi.org/10.3389/fpsyg.2020.575024.

Ferrante, Joan. "Correspondent: 'Blessed is the Speech of Your Mouth.'" In *Voice of the Living Light: Hildegard of Bingen and Her World*. Edited by Barbara Newman, 91–109. Berkeley: University of California Press, 1998.

Filthaut, E. M., OP, ed. *Henrich Seuse: Studien zum 600. Todestag, 1366–1966*. Köln: Albertus Magnus, 1966.

Fletcher, Christopher D. "The Customising Mindset in the Fifteenth Century: The Case of Newberry Inc. 1699." In *Customised Books in Early Modern Europe, 1400–1700*. Edited by Walter Melion and Christopher D. Fletcher, 41–64. Leiden: Brill, 2023.

——. "Reading Hildegard of Bingen's Letters." In *The Cambridge Companion to Hildegard of Bingen*. Edited by Jennifer Bain, 105–24. Cambridge: Cambridge University Press, 2021.

——. "Rhetoric, Reform, and Christian Eloquence: The Letter Form and the Religious Thought of Peter Damian." *Viator* 46, no. 1 (2015): 61–91.

——. *Tracking the Luther Controversy*. https://publications.newberry.org/luther-map/, accessed July 16, 2025.

——. "'Understand, Delight, and Obey': Religious Thought and the Letter Form, *c.* 1030–*c.* 1200." PhD diss., University of Chicago, 2015.

Folini, Christian. *Katharinental und Töss: Zwei mystische Zentren in sozialgeschichtlicher Perspektive*. Zürich: Chronos, 2007.

Freiburger Münsterbauverein, ed. *Das Freiburger Münster*. Regensburg: Schnell, 2011.

Gabriele, Matthew, and David M. Perry. *The Bright Ages: A New History of Medieval Europe*. New York: Harper, 2021.

Geary, Patrick. "What Happened to Latin?" *Speculum* 84, no. 4 (2009): 859–73.

Ginther, James. "Hildegard of Bingen's Theology." In *The Cambridge Companion to Hildegard of Bingen*. Edited by Jennifer Bain, 85–104. Cambridge: Cambridge University Press, 2021.

Gottschall, Dagmar. "Albert's Contributions to or Influence on Vernacular Literatures." In *A Companion to Albert the Great: Theology, Philosophy, and the Sciences*. Edited by Irven M. Resnick, 725–57. Leiden: Brill, 2013.

Gracia, Nahir Otaño. "Welcome to a New Reality! Reflections on the Medieval Academy of America's Panel: 'Inclusivity and Diversity: Challenges, Solutions, and Responses.'" *Medievalists of Color*, April 27, 2018. http://medievalistsofcolor.com/race-in-the-profession/welcome-to-a-new-reality-reflections-on-the-medieval-academy-of-americas-panel-inclusivity-and-diversity-challenges-solutions-and-responses/, accessed October 4, 2024.

Grollemond, Larisa and Bryan C. Keene. *The Fantasy of the Middle Ages: An Epic Journey through Imaginary Medieval Worlds*. Los Angeles: J. Paul Getty Museum, 2022.

Grubmüller, Klaus. "Die Viten der Schwestern von Töß und Elsbeth Stagel." *Zeitschrift für deutsches Altertum und deutsche Literatur* 98, no. 3 (1969): 171–204.

Grundmann, Herbert. "Die Frauen und die Literatur im Mittelalter: Ein Beitrag zur Frage nach der Entstehung des Schrifttums in der Volkssprache." *Archiv fiir Kulturgeschichte* 26 (1936): 129–61.

——. *Religiöse Bewegungen im Mittelalter: Untersuchungen über die geschichtlichen Zusammenhänge zwischen der Ketzerei, den Bettelorden und der religiösen Frauenbewegung im 12. und 13. Jahrhundert und über die geschichtlichen Grundlagen der deutschen Mystik*. 2nd ed. Hildesheim: Olms, 1961.

Haas, Alois. *Sermo mysticus: Studien zu Theologie und Sprache der deutschen Mystik*. Freiburg: Universitätsverlag, 1979.

Hall, Stuart. "Encoding and Decoding in the Television Discourse." *Essential Essays, Volume 1: Foundations of Cultural Studies*. Edited by David Morley, 257–76. New York: Duke University Press, 2018.

Hamburger, Jeffrey. "Medieval Self-Fashioning: Authorship, Authority, and Autobiography in Seuse's 'Exemplar.'" In *Christ Among the Medieval Dominicans: Representations of Christ in the Texts and Images of the Order of Preachers*. Edited by Kent Emery, Jr. and Joseph Wawrykow, 430–61. Notre Dame: University of Notre Dame Press, 1998.

——. "The Use of Images in the Pastoral Care of Nuns: The Case of Heinrich Suso and the Dominicans." *The Art Bulletin* 71, no. 1 (1989): 20–46.

Hanna, Ralph. "Vernacularity and Miscelleneity: Conditions of Literary Production in Late Medieval England." In *The Whole Book: Cultural Perspectives on the Medieval Miscellany*. Edited by Stephen G. Nichols and Siegfried Wenzel, 37–51. Ann Arbor: University of Michigan Press, 1996.

Heffernan, Thomas and E. Ann Matter, eds. *The Liturgy of the Medieval Church*. Kalamazoo: Medieval Institute, 2001.

Heng, Geraldine. *The Invention of Race in the European Middle Ages*. Cambridge: Cambridge University Press, 2018.

Hobbins, Daniel. *Authorship and Publicity Before Print: Jean Gerson and the Transformation of Late Medieval Learning*. Philadelphia: University of Pennsylvania Press, 2009.

Hoffman, Hartmut. "Zur mittelalterlichen Brieftechnik." In *Spiegel der Geschichte: Festgabe für Max Braubach*. Edited by Konrad Repgen and Stephan Skalweit, 141–70. Münster: Aschendorff, 1964.

Hohendahl, Peter Uwe. "Introduction to Reception Aesthetics." *New German Critique* 10 (1977): 29–63.

Howe, John. "The Nobility's Reform of the Medieval Church." *American Historical Review* 93 (1988): 317–39.

Hsy, Jonathan. *Antiracist Medievalisms: From "Yellow Peril" to Black Lives Matter*. Leeds: Arc Humanities, 2022.

——, and Julie Orlemanski. "Race and Medieval Studies: A Partial Bibliography." *postmedieval* 8 (2017): 500–31. Crowdsourced Google Doc version: https://docs.google.com/document/d/18JClsma1BMKYCxvgeWqwPej3ZSCrQXlAlXbL0CdqWmE/edit, accessed October 4, 2024.

Johnston, Michael. *The Middle English Book: Scribes and Readers, 1350–1500*. Oxford: Oxford University Press, 2023.

——, and Steven Van Dussen, eds. *The Medieval Manuscript Book: Cultural Approaches*. Cambridge: Cambridge University Press, 2015.

Kepplinger, Gretchin. "Rational Magic: Hypothesizing the Occult in Early Modern England with Newberry MS 5017, *The Book of Magical Charms*." MA thesis, University of Chicago, 2022.

Kieckhefer, Richard. *Unquiet Souls: Fourteenth-Century Saints and their Religious Milieu*. Chicago: University of Chicago Press, 1984.

Kienzle, Beverly, Debra L. Stoudt, and George Ferzoco, eds. *A Companion to Hildegard of Bingen*. Leiden: Brill, 2014.

——. *Hildegard of Bingen and her Gospel Homilies: Speaking New Mysteries*. Turnhout: Brepols, 2009.

Kim, Dorothy. "Teaching the Middle Ages in a Time of White Supremacy." *In the Middle*. Posted August 28, 2017. https://www.inthemedievalmiddle.com/2017/08/teaching-medieval-studies-in-time-of.html, accessed October 14, 2024.

Knight, Jeffrey Todd. "Organizing Manuscript and Print: From *compilatio* to Compilation." In *The Medieval Manuscript Book: Cultural Approaches*. Edited by Michael Johnston and Steven Van Dussen, 77–95. Cambridge: Cambridge University Press, 2015.

Kwakkel, Erik. "A New Type of Book for a New Type of Reader: The Emergence of Paper in Vernacular Book Production." *The Library* 7th ser., 4 (2003): 219–48.

Leclercq, Jean. *Saint Pierre Damien: Ermite et homme d'eglise*. Rome: Edizioni di storia e letterature, 1960.

Lerner, Robert. *The Heresy of the Free Spirit in the Later Middle Ages*. Berkeley: University of California Press, 1972.

Little, Lester K. "The Personal Development of Peter Damian." In *Order and Innovation in the Middle Ages: Essays in Honor of Joseph R. Strayer*. Edited by William C. Jordan, Bruce McNab, and Teofilo F. Ruiz, 317–41, 523–28. Princeton: Princeton University Press, 1976.

Lomuto, Sierra. "Public Medievalism and the Rigor of Anti-Racist Critique." *In the Middle*. Posted April 4, 2019. https://www.inthemedievalmiddle.com/2019/04/public-medievalism-and-rigor-of-anti.html, accessed October 15, 2024.

——. "White Nationalism and the Ethics of Medieval Studies." *In the Middle*. Posted December 5, 2016. https://www.inthemedievalmiddle.com/2016/12/white-nationalism-and-ethics-of.html, accessed October 15, 2024.

——, ed. "The Medieval Undone: Imagining a New Global Past." *boundary 2: an international journal of literature and culture* 50, no. 3 (2023).

McGinn, Bernard. *The Harvest of Mysticism in Late Medieval Germany (1300–1500)*. New York: Crossroad, 2005.

McKeon, Richard. "Rhetoric in the Middle Ages." *Speculum* 17 (1942), 1–32.

McKitterick, David. *Print, Manuscript and the Search for Order, 1450–1830*. Cambridge: Cambridge University Press, 2003.

Michel, Paul. "Heinrich Seuse als Diener des göttlichen Wortes: Persuasive Strategien bei der Verwendung von Bibelzitaten im Dienste seiner pastoralen Aufgaben." In *Das "einig ein": Studien zu Theorie und Sprache der deutschen Mystik*. Edited by Alois M. Haas and Heinrich Stirnimann, 281–367. Freiburg: Universitätsverlag, 1980.

Meconi, Honey. *Hildegard of Bingen*. Urbana: University of Illinois Press, 2018.

Miller, Tanya Stabler. *The Beguines of Medieval Paris: Gender, Patronage, and Spiritual Authority*. Philadelphia: University of Pennsylvania Press, 2014.

Molinelli-Stein, Barbara. "Seuse als Schriftsteller: Rhetorik und Rhythmus in seiner Prosa." PhD diss., Universität Tübingen, 1966.

Ndiaye, Noémie and Lia Markey, eds. *Seeing Race Before Race: Visual Culture and the Racial Matrix in the Premodern World*. Tempe: ACMRS, 2023.

Neddermeyer, Uwe. "*Radix studii et speculum vitae*: Verbreitung und Rezeption der Imitatio Christi in Handschriften und Drucken bis zur Reformation." In *Studien zum 15. Jahrhundert: Festschrift für Erich Meuthen*. Edited by Johannes Helmrath, 1:457–81. 2 vols. München: Oldenbourg, 1994.

New Catholic Encyclopedia. 15 vols. Washington, DC: Catholic University of America Press, 2003.

Newman, Barbara. "Hildegard of Bingen: Visions and Validations." *Church History* 54 (1985): 163–75.

——. *Sister of Wisdom: St. Hildegard's Theology of the Feminine*. 2nd ed. Berkeley: University of California Press, 1989.

——. "Sybil of the Rhine: Hildegard's Life and Times." In *Voice of the Living Light: Hildegard of Bingen and Her World*. Edited by Barbara Newman, 1–29. Berkeley: University of California Press, 1998.

——, ed. *Voice of the Living Light: Hildegard of Bingen and Her World*. Berkeley: University of California Press, 1998.

Ohly, Friedrich. *Sensus spiritualis: Studies of Medieval Significs and the Philology of Culture*. Edited by Samuel Jaffe. Translated by Kenneth Northcutt. Chicago: University of Chicago Press, 2005.

Palmer, Adrian. *Introduction to Marketing: Theory and Practice*. 3rd ed. Oxford: Oxford University Press, 2012.

Parkes, Malcom B. "The Literacy of the Laity." In *Literature and Western Civilization: The Mediaeval World*. Edited by David Daiches and Anthony Thorlby, 555–77. London: Aldus, 1973.

Perry, David and Cord J. Whitaker, eds. "The Ghosts of the Nineteenth Century and the Future of Medieval Studies." *postmedieval* 10, no. 2 (2019).

Peters, Ursula. *Religiöse Erfahrung als literarisches Faktum: Zur Vorgeschichte und Genese frauenmystischer Texte des 13. und 14. Jahrhunderts*. Tübingen: Niemeyer, 1988.

Petrucci, Armando. *Writers and Readers in Medieval Italy: Studies in the History of Written Culture*. Edited and translated by Charles M. Radding. New Haven: Yale University Press, 1995.

Ramos, Eduardo. "Confronting Whiteness: Antiracism in Medieval Studies." *postmedieval* 11 (2020): 493–502.

Ranft, Patricia. *The Theology of Peter Damian: Let Your Life Always Serve as a Witness*. Washington, DC: Catholic University of America Press, 2012.

Rankin, Susan. "Liturgical Drama." In *The New Oxford History of Music, Vol. 2: The Early Middle Ages to 1300*. Edited by Richard Crocker and David Hiley, 310–52. Oxford: Oxford University Press, 1990.

Reindel, Kurt. "Petrus Damiani und seine Korrespondenten." *Studi Gregoriani* 10 (1975): 203–19.

——. "Studien zur Überlieferung der Werke des Petrus Damiani." *Deutsches Archiv* 15 (1959): 23–102; 16 (1960): 73–154; and 18 (1962): 313–417.

Retucci, Fiorella. "Heinrich Seuse, Thomas Von Aquin und die 'Summa Theologiae Deutsch.'" *Recherches de théologie et philosophie médiévales* 77, no. 2 (2010): 283–97.

Rowe, Gene and Lynn J. Frewer. "A Typology of Public Engagement Mechanisms." *Science, Technology, and Human Values* 30, no. 2 (2005): 251–90.

Ruh, Kurt. *Die Mystik des deutschen Predigerordens und ihre Grundlegung durch die Hochscholastik*. München: Beck, 1996.

——, and Alois Haas. "Seuse, Heinrich, OP." In *Verfasserlexikon = Die deutsche Literature des Mittelalters: Verfasserlexikon*. Edited by Kurt Ruh et al., 8:1109–209. Berlin: De Gruyter, 1992.

Satterley, Renae. "Robert Ashley and the Authorship of Newberry MS 5017, The Book of Magical Charms." *Manuscript Studies: A Journal of the Schoenberg Institute for Manuscript Studies* 6, no. 2 (2021): 268–99.

Schrader, Marianna and Adelgundis Führkötter. *Die Echtheit des Schrifttums der hl. Hildegard von Bingen*. Köln: Böhlau, 1956.

Sedgman, Kirsty. "Audience Experience in an Anti-expert Age: A Survey of Theatre Audience Research." *Theatre Research International* 42, no. 3 (2018): 307–22.

——. *The Reasonable Audience: Theatre Etiquette, Behaviour Policing, and the Live Performance Experience*. New York: Palgrave, 2018.

Spadafora, David et al. *The Newberry 125: Stories from Our Collection*. Chicago: The Newberry Library, 2012.

Thompson, James Westfall. *The Literacy of the Laity in the Middle Ages*. New York: Franklin, 1960.

Tipka, Ernst. "Subjekt und Text: Nonnenviten und Offenbarungsliteratur in Frauenklöstern des 14. Jahrhunderts." *Mediaevistik* 2 (1989): 225–53.

Tobin, Frank. "Henry Suso and Elsbeth Stagel: Was the Vita a Cooperative Effort?" In *Gendered Voices: Medieval Saints and Their Interpreters*. Edited by Catherine M. Mooney: 118–35. Philadelphia: University of Pennsylvania Press, 1999.

Van Acker, Lieven. "Der Briefwechsel der heiligen Hildegard von Bingen. Vorbemerkungen zu einer kritischen Edition." *Revue bénédictine* 98, nos. 1–2 (1988): 141–68; 99 (1989): 118–54.

Van Engen, John. "Letters and the Public Persona of Hildegard." In *Hildegard von Bingen in ihrem historischen Umfeld: Internationaler wissenschaftlicher Kongreß zum 900jährigen Jubiläum, 13.–19. September 1998, Bingen am Rhein*. Edited by Alfred Haverkamp, 375–418. Mainz: Von Zabern, 2000.

——. "Letters, Schools, and Written Culture in the Eleventh and Twelfth Century." In *Dialektik und Rhetorik im frühen und hohen Mittelalter: Rezeption, Überlieferung und gesellschaftliche Wirkung antiker Gelehrsamkeit vornehmlich im 9. und 12. Jahrhundert*. Edited by Johannes Fried, 97–132. München: Oldenbourg, 1997.

——. *Sisters and Brothers of the Common Life: The Devotio moderna and the World of the Later Middle Ages*. Philadelphia: University of Pennsylvania Press, 2008.

Verfasserlexikon = Die deutsche Literature des Mittelalters: Verfasserlexikon. Edited by Kurt Ruh et al. 14 vols. Berlin: De Gruyter, 1978–2008.

Von Moos, Peter. *Geschichte als Topik: Das rhetorische Exemplum von der Antike zur Neuzeit und die "historiae" im Policraticus Johanns von Salisbury*. ORDO: Studien zur Literatur und Gesellschaft des Mittelalters und der frühen Neuzeit 2. New York: Olms, 1988.

Whitaker, Cord J. *Black Metaphors: How Modern Racism Emerged from Medieval Race-Thinking*. Philadelphia: University of Pennsylvania Press, 2019.

——, Nahir I. Otaño Gracia, and François-Xavier Fauvelle, eds. "Race, Race-Thinking, and Identity in the Global Middle Ages." Special issue, *Speculum* 99, no. 2 (2024).

Williams-Krapp, Werner. "Henry Suso's *Vita* between Mystagogy and Hagiography." In *Seeing and Knowing: Women and Learning in Medieval Europe 1200–1550*. Edited by Anneke B. Mulder-Bakker, 35–47. Turnhout: Brepols, 2004.

Zátonyi, Maura. *Vidi et intellexi: die Schrifthermeneutik in der Visionstrilogie Hildegards von Bingen*. Münster: Aschendorff, 2012.

INDEX